Hawking
with
Golden Eagles

To Dave
an HO Rott

To Tonya
for being so understanding
and patient.

Hawking with Golden Eagles

Martin Hollinshead

hancock

house

ISBN 0-88839-343-1
Copyright © 1995 Martin Hollinshead

Cataloging in Publication Data
Hollinshead, Martin, 1959-
    Hawking with Golden Eagles
    ISBN 0-88839-343-1

    1. Falconry. 2. Golden eagle. I. Title.
SK321.H66 1995 799.2'32 C95-910644-8

Editor: Barbara Brown
Production: Myron Shutty and Nancy Kerr
Cover design: Karen Whitman
Cover painting and previous page illustration: V. Gorbatov

Published simultaneously in Canada and the United States by

HANCOCK HOUSE PUBLISHERS LTD.
19313 Zero Avenue, Surrey, B.C. V4P 1M7
(604) 538-1114   Fax (604) 538-2262

HANCOCK HOUSE PUBLISHERS
1431 Harrison Avenue, Blaine, WA 98230-5005
(604) 538-1114   Fax (604) 538-2262

Contents

Preface

My purpose in writing this small book is to try to give an insight into hawking with golden eagles. These raptors have frequently been described in less-than-glowing terms and their value as modern day falconry birds questioned. This book will attempt to paint a more positive picture. Naturally, when flown under unsuitable conditions and handled by inexperienced falconers, golden eagles will give a poor account of themselves. But, if trained and flown correctly, these eagles can be employed very effectively by the contemporary falconer and provide him with a unique hawking experience.

My own understanding and appreciation of the golden eagle owes little to my early British falconry background. Far more influential have been my central European experiences. I have spent a good deal of time living and hawking on the Continent. There, my involvement with three large falconry centers has resulted in me being presented with opportunities seldom afforded the private individual; and, with Germany or Austria serving as a base, I have traveled widely and hunted with golden eagles in many different parts of Europe.

In writing this book, I have assumed that those interested in hawking with golden eagles will already have a background of experience with birds such as goshawks, Harris' hawks, or red-tailed hawks. Let me stress that a golden eagle is definitely no bird for a novice falconer. With this in mind, I deemed it unnecessary to cover very basic falconry topics in any detail. Comments on the more rudimentary aspects of the sport have been restricted to where I feel they are truly required. I have written very much with the practicing falconer in mind. However, I have also tried to produce a text that will be found readable and informative by those perhaps not directly involved in practical falconry, but who have an interest in some related topic. It is hoped that this book will be of value to anyone keen to discover just what these magnificent birds are capable of as trained hunting allies.

Acknowledgements

In writing this book I have needed to call on the help of many friends. My thanks go to: Andreas Zechmeister, Jürgen Färber, Thomas Dollmann, Josef Kubec, Ron Moore, Mike Clowes and Martin and Jan Rinik. For helping with additional photographs I would also like to thank: T. Large, L. Uhlir, T. Anderle, J. Frankhouser, R. Emminger and U. Reich. For the cover illustration and the sketch of the Kazakh falconer I owe a debt of gratitude to V. Gorbatov.

A special acknowledgement must go to Josef Hiebeler for his help and encouragement regarding this project.

1 The Golden Eagle

Although this book concerns itself primarily with the golden eagle as a falconry bird, a brief look at the wild-living eagle is fairly essential and so it is with this that I will begin this first chapter.

The golden eagle (*Aquila chrysaetos*) is one of ten "booted" eagles that make up the genus *Aquila*. All are medium to large birds of prey, but only one other member of the genus, Verreaux's eagle (*Aquila verreauxi*), can in any way be compared to the golden eagle in terms of sheer flying and hunting ability. It is also worth noting that these two species, together with a third, the wedge-tailed eagle (*Aquila audax*), possess much larger feet and talons than any other of the *Aquila* eagles.

The golden eagle has a huge distributon. Holarctic, it is found in the New World south to Mexico and across Europe and Asia south to North Africa and the Himalayas. A number of sub-species have been described, but the most widely recognized are *A.c. homeryi*, *A.c. daphanea*, *A.c. canadensis* and *A.c. japonica*. Over most of its range the golden eagle is essentially a bird of wild, uneven landscapes, avoiding extensive flat terrain or areas of agricultural development. The more rugged the terrain, the better *chrysaetos* fares.

In the Old World, suitable habitat occurs in a variety of forms. Of great interest are the areas of uninhabited, flat forest frequented by eagles in parts of Scandinavia and European Russia. Here, hunting is done over open, but equally level, ground. More typical locations are seen in Scotland where vast, open hill country is available. Spain too, offers ample broken terrain and, as with Scotland, at relatively low elevation. But in many parts of Europe, human encroachment has forced the eagle out of its lower lying haunts, and in central Europe it has become a true mountain species of high altitude settings. East of the Volga, in a huge sweep through central Asia, Siberia, Mongolia and northern China, *chrysaetos* has access to true wilderness country. In North America, especially the western United States, it finds equally favorable conditions; landscapes made up of mountain and hill ranges, desolate plateaus and river gorges.

In the more northerly parts of its range the golden Eagle can be considered migratory with some birds migrating in the true sense of the word. However, some populations do not migrate latitudinally at all and simply move to lower ground for the winter. Such populations would include Scottish eagles and the Alpine birds of Switzerland, Austria, and Germany (Bavaria). In North America there is a large autumn flow south to Mexico. This migration, taking place in the west, is well documented, yet, many eagles remain in cold northern regions and the movement of these birds is not fully understood.

The golden eagle does not possess the weight and dimensions of the very largest eagles, but, with a length of 760 to 970 millimeters and a wingspan of up to approximately 2300 millimeters, it is still a sizable raptor. Not surprisingly for such a widespread species, there can be a marked difference in size between individual birds, depending on from where they originate. Generally speaking, the largest golden eagles are those from central Asia and eastern Siberia. The smallest birds are found in Korea and Japan. But wherever they originate from, females are always larger than their corresponding males. Build is another feature worth drawing attention to. This can alter somewhat from bird to bird, some can appear thick set and powerful, others quite slim and fine. Of special interest are the feet. In all golden eagles they are, as noted, large, but, as with body shape, the length and width of toes can vary quite noticeably. This means that birds of equal weight will not always possess feet of the same caliber.

As with size and weight, some variation in color is seen in golden eagles (all sub-species being darker than *A.c. chrysaetos*), but nothing that could be considered dramatic. At a distance, the adult bird appears to be a fairly uniform darkish brown. On closer inspection, one notices subtle areas of "shading" and the golden tint or hue of the nape feathers (this is not always pronounced), but there is no plumage feature that immediately draws the eye. First-year birds are darker, and, when perched, can in fact appear almost black. This caused some early observers to question the identity of young birds. When seen in flight there is little room for confusion. Now the dark base plumage contrasts vividly with large white areas on wings and tail. This immature coloring is lost slowly with the bold white areas receding and the plumage becoming gradually lighter. True adult plumage is first acquired at five to six years of age. This applies to both male and female eagles, for their is no plumage difference between the sexes, their appearance is the same. The feet and cere are yellow, the beak and talons black; and the legs are, as with all *Aquila* eagles, completely feathered (hence the term "booted").

Golden eagles reach breeding age at about five years and once paired they bond for life. A pair will normally have several nests in their territory and each year select one for use. In some areas, cliffs and rock faces are always preferred, while in other parts of its range, tree nests are quite common. With the eagles' repeated use, the repairing of a nest and the adding of materials can result in huge structures.

Two eggs are normally laid and the time of year when this occurs depends on where, geographically speaking, the breeding territory is situated. In Mexico and North Africa, dates are given as early as January; and in the far north, eggs are laid as late as June. In temperate Europe and North America, March is the significant month. Incubation requires forty-three to forty-five days and is carried out mainly by the female. The eggs, laid at intervals, hatch in sequence and, in the majority (approximately 80 percent) of cases where two young hatch, the older chick ends up killing its sibling.

The young eagle makes its first flight at about seventy-five days old, but will remain close to the nest for several weeks after this. Just how long young golden eagles are dependent on their parents after leaving the nest is not clear.

Much of the country inhabited by the golden eagle would be well suited to a "watch and wait" approach to hunting, but this is not its way. It much prefers to hunt actively on the wing, using lift along ridges and hillsides to aid it in its search for food. Attacks on prey vary from those made in a quick opportunistic way to those involving a degree of pre-planning. To successfully hunt animals that seek refuge underground when threatened, a calculated approach is always necessary. At such times the eagle will often feign disinterest, flying leisurely away to finally disappear behind some hill or irregularity in the landscape. But the quarry's postion will have been marked and as soon as the eagle knows it is out of sight, a concealed hunting approach will be made. What form this takes will be decided in relation to the terrain. Attacks are frequently low-level and, with the altitude of the initial searching soar lost, the eagle uses undulations in the land to cloak its approach. In towering mountian country the final stages can be very dramatic with hte eagle flashing past rocky crags and pinnacles as it closes on a still unsuspecting victim. When pursuing prey that, once on the move, more typically relies on its speed and maneuverability to avoid capture (hares, for example), the element of surprise is less vital—though always desirable. The most spectacular attacks are those made by high, soaring eagles to exposed and vulnerable prey. The bird commits itself to an often very steep and fast dive, sometimes coming in vertically from above.

The golden eagle is orientated very much to mammalian prey and, although it will take anything from reptiles to upland game birds, mammals such as hares, rabbits and rodents of various types are normally favored. Foxes not infrequently fall prey to golden eagles and the young of various "hoofed" animals are also taken; even the adults of the smaller species are sometimes vulnerable. These are normally single bird assaults, but attacks on deer and antelope involving two or even three eagles have been recorded. Although such occurences are rare, they do highlight a less well known side of the eagle's nature. Two bird pursuits of smaller prey are more frequently observed. For instance, in the European Alps, the husky Alpine marmot, a favorite quarry, is sometimes hunted this way.

When dealing with large mammalian prey, the golden eagles' habit is to be direct and forceful. The victim is bound to immediately. When the eagle does not follow an assualt through then this will have been due to some type of natural obstruction or the animal managing to dodge or hide. It is not the golden eagle's manner to harry its victim or try and wear it down. This does not mean to say that if thwarted, the bird will not make a follow-up attack. If it sees an opportunity it will. Once actually taken hold of, large animals may well fight and struggle. But this type of physical confrontation is something nature has equipped the golden eagle to deal with. Being extremely tough, and blessed with remarkably resilient plumage, the bird is able to weather truly furious encounters. Still struggling, the prey is brought under control by the eagle's strong feet and legs. The legs are surprisingly long and give their owner substantial reach. This is put to good use when subduing quarry on the ground. The mortal damage is done by the power of the eagle's huge feet driving the long hind and front-inside talons deep into vital organs. This deadly grip is maintained until the victim expires. Smaller mammals can sustain frightful skeletal damage, with major bones being completely broken and rib cages crushed.

When it needs to be, the golden eagle can be very effective against winged prey and, in some parts of its range, *chrysaetos* takes a considerable number of grouse and ptarmigan. This is especially the case in areas where suitable mammals are not available or are in limited supply. Swift-flying game birds are particularly vulnerable when on the ground, but they can be caught by eagles even when in flight. Compared to this, the golden eagle's willingness to feed on carrion seems a very sharp contrast. Yet in some regions, carrion is an important source of food for golden eagles during the winter months. Scottish eagles, those of the Alps and the North American birds that spend their winters at high latitudes, all, to a greater or lesser degree, rely on carrion. In the Alps, winter carrion helps resident eagles balance the loss of the Alpine marmot. During the winter this animal hibernates and so is not available.

Robbing other raptors of their kills is another tactic employed by golden eagles in an effort to secure food. Although not as piratical as some species, this type of behavior is quite normal for golden eagles and it can have serious consequences for the other bird of prey involved. Hawks and falcons themselves do sometimes fall victim to golden eagles and a substantial number of falconers' birds have been killed by eagles. This can quite easily happen when a trained falcon is down on quarry some way from the hawking party.

The Golden Eagle and Falconry

Traditionally, the golden eagle is a bird of central Asian falconry and its association with the peoples of central Asia is a lengthy one; indeed, this partnership is probably as old as falconry itself. It may be that the northern hemisphere falcons of the Old World and the goshawk were experimented with before the golden eagle, but surely this magnificent species must have aroused man's curiosity from very early on.

A variety of quarries have been taken by trained golden eagles in Asia, but, historically, this big raptor was prized for flights to large animals such as saiga antelope, gazelle, roe deer, fox and even wolf. Marco Polo witnessed this kind of hawking during the latter part of the thirteenth century whilst in the service of Kubilai Khan and the records of many early travelers mention eagles being used for falconry.

For detailed descriptions, however, one has to come forward in time to the 1800s when accounts such as the one given by J. Biddulph were published. This is what he had to say:

"I also saw the burgoots, or trained eagles, kill gazelles and foxes. I was not fortunate enough to see them kill a wolf, though they were twice flown; but the animals on both occasions being in thick bush jungle and at a great distance, the birds did not sight them. Their owners, however, spoke of it as an ordinary occurrence.

"When the jungle is not high, they sight their prey at a great distance and sweep up to it without any apparent effort however fast it may be going. Turning suddenly when over its head, they strike it with unerring aim. If a fox, they grasp its throat with their powerful talons and seize it round the muzzle with the other foot, keeping the jaws closed with an iron grip so that the animal is powerless. From the great ease with which an eagle disposes of a full-grown fox, I could see that a wolf would have no better chance."

Biddulph's account is most interesting; however, he assumed a little too much regarding wolf hawking. One finds references to eagles being maimed, and even killed, by wolves and these flights must always have contained an element of risk. Nevertheless, some eagles did become extremely competent at catching wolves and had substantial tallies to their credit.

For wolf hawking, only the largest female eagles were used, males being reserved for less hazardous quarries. But whatever sex the eagle and whatever the quarry, hawking was nearly always conducted from horseback.

The horse is in fact a recurring theme when one digs into the history of eagle falconry. Used not only as a means of transport and hunting aid, horses and ponies were sometimes relied on to provide meat, milk and even clothing. The hardy Bashkir pony is a good example of the kind of animal used. Evolving around the southern foothills of the Ural mountains, its thick coat could be spun into cloth and it provided an ample supply of milk. In fact, the Russian drink of *kumiss* (fermented mare's milk) came from the Bashkir people.

Bashkir falconers do not come immediately to mind when one thinks of the golden eagle, but that they once flew eagles there seems little doubt. One finds old references to this effect and Mr. Constantine Haller of St. Petersburg, who traveled to Bashkiria in the 18OOs, recorded quite specifically that Bashkir falconers flew eagles. His report actually mentioned both Kirghiz and Bashkir falconers. It is perhaps worth noting that, on his return from Bashkiria, Haller brought a trained eagle back with him.

While there may be room for discussion regarding exactly which falconers have utilized the golden eagle, this bird's strong connection with horse-riding peoples is beyond question. Several authors have described eagles being flown from the saddle and T.W. Atkinson, writing in the 1860s, conjures up a vivid picture of a mounted hawking expedition in the following quotation:

"Soon after daybreak we were all up and making preparations for our departure. Horses were standing ready saddled and everything indicated a busy scene. I saw two Kirghis occupied with Bearcoote and the falcon. Having finished our morning meal, horses were brought for the Sultan and myself. I was to be mounted today on one of his best steeds, a fine dark gray that stood champing my English bit, which he did not appear to relish. All my party were mounted on the Sultan's horses, ours had been sent on to the aoul, with a party of his people and three of my Kalmucks. When mounted, I had time to examine the party. The Sultan and his two sons rode beautiful animals. The eldest boy carried the falcon which was to fly at the feathered game; a well mounted Kirghis held the Bearcoote, chained to a perch, which was secured into a socket on his saddle. The eagle had shackles and a hood and was perfectly quiet; he was under the charge of two men. Near to the Sultan were his three hunters, or guards, with their rifles and around us were a band of about twenty Kirghis in their bright-colored kalats. More than half the number were a wild-looking group whom people would rather behold at a distance than come into contact with."

But wild-looking or not, it was in the company of these horsemen that Atkinson experienced some fine sport, seeing deer and antelope taken.

For a taste of the hawking he enjoyed, let us pick up his account after one deer has been killed and as the party continues with their hunt:

"We had not gone far before a herd of small antelopes were seen feeding on the plain. Again the bird soared up in circles—this time, I thought, to a greater elevation—and again he made the fatal swoop at his intended victim and the animal was dead before we reached him. The Bearcoote is unerring in his flight; unless the animal pursued can escape into holes in the rocks, as the fox does sometimes, death is his certain doom."

It is worth noting that Atkinson's "Bearcoote" and Biddulph's "burgoot" were both golden eagles. This is the only large species

16

historically associated with the once primarily nomadic peoples of central Asia and the references one sometimes comes across to other species, such as the imperial eagle and steppe eagle, being used are not well substantiated. Whether referred to as Bearcoote, burgoot, Berkute, or Berkut, the bird in question will be a golden eagle.

But what of the golden eagle's falconry history in the west? Well in truth, this species has no traditional ties with European falconry, and, although the book of St. Albans clearly states "an eagle for an emperor," the love central Asian chieftains and rulers had for the golden eagle was never shared by their European counterparts. As Harting points out in his *Hints on the Management of Hawks and Practical Falconry*, even French kings, such as Henry IV and Louis XIII, who practiced falconry with great enthusiasm, avoided eagles. From time to time, eagles were kept, but more as curiosities than anything else and the serious hawking one sees being done with the golden eagle today in parts of Europe is a relatively recent development.

Just how the eagle gained acceptance in European falconry circles is difficult to chart with any accuracy. Nevertheless, one has to acknowledge the work done by several individuals. A falconer who certainly deserves recognition is Fritz Loges, who, between 1937 and 1955, flew eagles very successfully in Germany. Another pioneer of some note was George Lelovich, an east European falconer who began to use an eagle for hare hawking in Hungary in 1940. Then, of course, there is Friedrich Remmler, whose falconry experiences prior to the second world war included wolf hawking. But it was not until the mid 1960s and later that the golden eagle's ability was brought to a wider audience. During this period, a small number of eagles were being flown, by Claus Fentzloff and others, at falconry gatherings in Germany and Austria. The impressive performances they gave did not go unnoticed. These birds were being used primarily as hare hawks, and, for this type of falconry, they were proving to be very effective.

During the late 1970s and through the 1980s, golden eagles were to be seen at most of the larger falconry field meetings; and the former Czechoslovakia became especially popular with eagle enthusiasts. Here, there were brown hares in densities to exceed even the numbers found on some of the open arable land of Lower Austria and spacious, welcoming landscapes to fly over. At these meetings, eagle owners from various parts of Europe came together to share experiences and to show those who had never seen an eagle in action just what a good golden eagle was capable of.

From the mid-1980s onwards, international falconry meetings in Hungary were to play a part in exposing the eagle's talents. With the promise of ideal hawking country and again, an abundance of quarry, these also attracted eagle owners, one meeting drawing a falconer from as far away as Siberia. Poland, too, has been host to hawking meets that have seen golden eagles present. However, it is definitely to some of the meetings in the former Czechoslovakia one should look if evidence of the golden eagle's acceptance and value is required. At an international field meeting in 1992, no less than twenty-eight golden eagles were registered.

In North America, the situation regarding golden eagles is slightly different. Although eagles have been used in the United States and Canada, falconers who have achieved any degree of success with these birds have been few and far between. Not so many years ago, there seemed to be an interest developing in golden eagles and falconry journals often contained letters and comments regarding eagles. One or two individuals seemed to be working toward having the eagle become recognized as a North American falconry bird, albeit in a small way. But in more recent years, there has been very little activity in this area. That said, there have been those who have done fine work with golden eagles and Morlan Nelson is perhaps the best known North American eagle devotee. This man has spent many years flying eagles. He is respected across the continent, not only as an authority on golden eagles, but also for his field study and film work in general.

Why golden eagles are not more widely utilized in North America is difficult to say. Perhaps North American falconry has been influenced by things being done in Britain (and vice versa). British and North American falconers certainly enjoy many similar interests and a shared language has resulted in much interaction. An obvious example of this is seen with New World hunting birds, such as the Harris' hawk and red-tailed hawk, which have become established birds of British falconry. However, for those interested in golden eagles, this collaboration has had a less than positive result. When discussing golden eagles, one has to isolate Britain from continental Europe and deal with the topic separately. Eagles are employed far less frequently in Britain than they are in central Europe and are less well understood.

It seems likely that some of the negative references to eagles found in British hawking literature have influenced the way North American falconers view these birds. Even in quite modern publications (both British and North American), one finds golden eagles described as undesirable. Whatever the reasons may be, the absence of golden eagles in North American falconry circles is a great pity. Canada and the United States are both rich with suitable hawking country and are home to a variety of viable quarries.

2   Choice of Bird

As we have seen, the golden eagle has long been used by the falconers of central Asia and its value as a hunting bird is beyond question. Nevertheless, any modern European or North American falconer should think very carefully indeed before committing himself to the task of flying a golden eagle. The word "task" makes eagle ownership sound like some kind of punishment, but that is exactly what it can end up being if all of the necessary ingredients for a worthwhile experience are not there at the outset. The falconer will need to have an abundance of suitable quarry, fitting landscapes to fly over, a background of experience with goshawks or buteos and he will also need time. If an eagle is to do really well in off-the-fist-type flights, then it will need to be kept extremely fit; and this will require a carefully regulated training program.

Exactly what constitutes "suitable quarry" will be looked at in a later chapter, but it is fairly obvious that the falconer who can only guarantee flights to European rabbits or North American cottontails would be far better off with perhaps a Harris' hawk or goshawk. Describing suitable hawking locations is not an easy thing to do, for the golden eagle is a little less restricting in this respect than many might imagine. One does not need vast prairie-type landscapes. Open, unrestricted agricultural ground is quite acceptable (a well-trained eagle will even fly in woodland), but this is not a species to be flown in enclosed country criss-crossed with wire fences, dissected by roads and dotted with small holdings and farms. Areas of low human population are always desirable.

The Choice Between Male and Female Eagle

When it comes to choosing between the sexes of the more commonly flown falconry species, the decision normally revolves around the available quarry. Often, the male of the species has not really got the weight and strength to deal with the larger, or what might be the more commonly pursued, quarries. A good example of this is seen with European goshawks, where the female is nearly always preferred. With golden eagles, the choice between male and female is less frequently decided in relation to quarry. An average-sized male will take all of the more commonly hunted animals and the female only has something additional to offer when the falconer is going to concentrate on pursuing large quarry.

Also, it should be noted that the sexes differ in terms of temperament. The difficulties of working with female eagles are often overstated, but it is certainly true to say that females require very careful handling and should only be considered by the most experienced of falconers.

Weight is another consideration. If the eagle is being flown from the fist, then the greater weight of a female can make a big difference on a long day. With a little practice, most falconers manage quite well with a male eagle, but a female takes a lot of getting used to. There are, of course, large and small examples of both sexes and here would seem a suitable place to look at flying weights. Males fly from about 2650 grams to 3800 grams, with a normal range of 3150 grams to 3300 grams. Females fly from 3600 grams to 4600 grams (possibly even 4800 grams), with the normal range falling between 4100 grams and 4400 grams. From time to time, falconers mention birds flying lighter or heavier than this, but here I have restricted myself to quoting figures from personal experience.

Other Considerations

In addition to the decision between male and female eagle, the falconer will also need to consider the bird's background. Tradition-

21

ally, one would be thinking in terms of acquiring a bird from the wild, but, today, eagles bred in captivity are quite available. Indeed, for many falconers, captive-bred birds represent the only legal option when it comes to acquiring and retaining a golden eagle for falconry purposes.

If the eagle is coming from a captive-breeding program, then a hand-reared bird should be considered preferable to one that has been reared in some other way; and a hand-reared eagle is always more desirable, from a falconry point of view, than one that has been totally parent-reared in a seclusion-type breeding chamber. The hand-reared eagle requires no actual taming (as its parent-reared counterpart would), is bold and biddable and becomes strongly bonded to its trainer. If reared and handled correctly, this bird is a true joy to fly. Even when dealing with wild-taken birds, my first choice would be an eyas taken at about twenty days old, rather than an eagle trapped after it had left the nest (or indeed acquired at the brancher stage). If the eagle is coming from a hawk breeder, then the falconer may find himself being given less say regarding at what age he obtains the bird. However, age is not so critical, as long as the young eagle in question is definitely being hand-reared and is enjoying plenty of activity around it. In fact, if the falconer cannot guarantee sufficiently busy scenes at home, his bird might well be better off with the breeder. That said, I would strongly recommend taking delivery of the young eagle long before it can actually fly. The reason for this is that, unlike the more conventional procedure that would see the bird only taken up for training once fully feathered and hard-penned, with eyas eagles, the training begins much sooner.

The aggression and general bad manners so often associated with hand-reared birds (or to be more precise, birds that have been incorrectly hand reared), would no doubt be a serious concern for many falconers contemplating working with a golden eagle. But, if correctly reared and trained, the eyas eagle will not be a constant danger to its owner or other people in general. Nevertheless, golden eagles are big, powerful birds, and, whatever the background of the bird in question, it should be handled with the utmost care and respect.

Aware that many readers would find my liking for hand-reared eagles difficult to understand (and my account of the bird perhaps even unbelievable), I felt it would be a good idea to include a few supporting comments from someone else. To this end, I asked Mike Clowes of Great Britain to voice his feelings on the subject. Mr. Clowes is a respected and experienced falconer and chairman of the Welsh Hawking Club. From a letter Mr. Clowes kindly supplied, I quote:

"When I began to practice falconry in 1967 there were few golden eagles being flown in Britain. Those that were had been taken from the wild under license and everything possible was done to prevent imprinting. If you asked an eagle owner how old an eaglet had to be before it was taken you were invariably told to wait until just before it left the nest. The later you left it the better. Under no circumstances were you to take a 'downie' and hand rear it. This was taboo and horror stories were rife about the damage done to falconers by eagles that were taken too young.

"It was with this background that in 1988 I attended an international field meeting in Hungary. There I was amazed to see Austrian and German falconers flying golden eagles which had been deliberately hand-reared. The first thing that was noticeable was the close bond between eagle and falconer. The quarry was hare and if the eagle missed, it would often bank over and return straight to its handler's fist—very impressive. Also, there was absolutely no fuss when a hare was caught. The falconer moved in, dispatched the quarry and tempted the eagle onto the fist for a tidbit. These birds came off kills without any trouble at all and within a couple of minutes were ready for another flight.

"In 1992 I was a guest at a large falconry meeting in Opocno, Czechoslovakia. There I met the author and one of his German colleagues. Both were flying hand-reared golden eagles and the behavior of these birds (and others at the meeting) reinforced the favorable impression I had gained in Hungary. There is no doubt in my mind that, with the right kind of rearing and training, a hand-reared eagle has an awful lot to offer."

3 Equipment, Housing and Transport

The basic equipment used with golden eagles does not differ significantly from that used with other hunting birds. Nevertheless, one or two areas do need commenting on and so a glance at equipment, housing and transport is required.

Jesses, Swivels, Bells and Perches

All too often one sees golden eagles wearing jesses which are excessively long. The idea behind these jesses seems to be that they make the handling of the bird easier. However, massive jesses are certainly not required when working with correctly trained eagles. As a guide to length, when laid out flat the jesses for an average-size male eagle will measure (individually) approximately 45 cm from end to end.

A question that often arises is whether or not aylmeri anklets and slitless flying jesses are essential when hunting with golden eagles. I feel they are not as important as when working with smaller birds, but even an eagle can get snagged by the swivel slits in traditional jesses. It is worth noting that some of the eagle jesses used by central Asian falconers resemble aylmeri jesses more closely than the traditional European type. These Asian jesses comprise of an anklet and a long, plaited leather jess. The main difference is that the jess is permanently attached to the anklet.

Naturally one of the main considerations when making jesses for an eagle is the bird's strength but it is also vitally important that the jesses be supple and fit well. Poorly fitting jesses will result in the leg feathers becoming worn and can even lead to sore legs. Also, jesses should be put on with the smooth side of the leather against the bird's leg. This too will help reduce wear and tear on leg feathers.

Every care should be taken to protect the eagle's legs, for example, when I have a pair of traditional jesses to fit I never put them straight on to the eagle. I thread each jess together as if it were on the bird and then work at the anklet end with my fingers. My main concern is to mould them so that they casually bend over forming a rounded, rather than sharp, edge. If made correctly, the top and bottom edges of a traditional jess will contain a multitude of small cuts (creating a fringe) to help them fold over. But if the jess is fitted directly to the bird one can not guarantee that these cuts will soften the edge sufficiently. It is a much better idea to make the jesses up and form them manually. The area most deserving of special attention is where the jess comes together at the back of the leg. The finished article will actually look comfortable and have a supple, almost worn look about it. Needless to say, the leather will need to be dressed with oil, but the anklet end should not be greased inside, again due to the bird's feathered legs. Once fitted, jesses should be checked at regular intervals.

In an effort to avoid or correct problems I once experimented with modifying aylmeri jesses. My aim was to construct a jess with the softest edge possible. To achieve this I lined a standard aylmeri anklet with a lighter piece of leather which was slightly wider. The pieces were glued rough side to rough side with adhesive purchased for the purpose. Then, the protruding edges of the lining were folded over forming wide, rounded cuffs, top and bottom of the anklet. These were glued firmly down. After being trimmed and formed by hand these jesses were tested with excellent results on a male eagle who had suffered some leg feather wear.

The bells for golden eagles should not be too large; and I totally disagree with the idea that the bigger the bird, the bigger its bells should be. Large leg bells look unsightly and are completely unnecessary. Some of the small hawk and falcon bells now available are quite adequate for an eagle. I tend to use just one leg bell, and, when it is of small size, I prefer to attach this (with a cable-tie) to the rear of the aylmeri anklet, or where a traditional jess comes together. Attaching a leg bell in this way, rather than using a traditional bewit, again helps reduce the wear on leg feathers. Telemetry transmitters are tail-mounted in the normal way.

Suitable eagle swivels can be found in either a standard figure eight or "D" shape. Naturally, these should be made from stainless steel. Another option is to use a snap-clip and swivel on each jess, these being joined at the leash. One sees this arrangement used more frequently with falcons, but, if allowances are made for the increase in size, it can also work quite well with eagles. A drawback, however, is that the clips add to the overall length of the jesses and can cause these to get fouled up on blocks and perches. To counter this, additional slits should be made further up the jesses if snap-clips are to be used for even a short period of time.

Blocks and perches need to be substantial and well made. Like other raptors, eagles feel more secure (especially toward evening) when sitting fairly high up, but from a practical point of view and to reduce the risk of injury to the bird, perches must be kept as low as possible. Here, a compromise will have to be met and a block with a height of fifty centimeters should prove satisfactory for both man and bird. The top of the block (which should be rounded, rather than flat) will need to be at least thirty centimeters across to prevent the jesses from straddling it; and, as a surface, thick, "lumpy" rubber is hard to beat.

Ring-perches have a reputation for being tail destroyers, but if kept fairly low to the ground, they can be used successfully with eagles. They will need to have a diameter of something like fifty centimeters and be padded to a circumference of approximately twenty-five centimeters.

From a safety point of view, bow-perches are excellent. They allow the use of a short leash, thus reducing the strain on the bird's legs during a bate and any kind of tangle involving jesses or leash is almost completely ruled out.

Gloves and Hoods

For early training sessions, a good thick glove is required and the use of a light leather oversleeve for the upper arm is also worth considering. A decent glove is essential when working with young, inexperienced eagles as, when they land on the fist, they tend to grip tightly. As things progress and the eagle becomes more accomplished at flying and landing (and settles down into training routines), a heavy glove is really not necessary, and, for hawking, a relatively light glove can be used.

It has been suggested that a young bird might first be called to a garnished T-perch held in both hands and then transferred to the fist after it has eaten and relaxed. This is an interesting idea, but the use of such a device is certainly not essential and eagles can be flown to and from the fist from the word go as long as care is taken.

The use of a T-perch is nothing new: eagles have been carried on and flown from perches for centuries; and one does not have to delve too deeply into falconry or the older Asian travel literature to find evidence of the fact. That said, the use of a perch has never been the standard or only method of transporting eagles in central Asia. Golden eagles were (and still are) frequently flown from the fist by mounted falconers, the falconer's arm resting on a crutch supported by the horse's saddle.

Arm supports of various types are available in Europe, but they cannot really be considered important for falconers hunting on foot. They often prove to be more of an encumbrance than a help in the field.

From the superfluous to the essential: hoods. Many falconers fly eagles very successfully without ever using hoods, but I feel that, whenever possible, golden eagles should be hood trained. It is often desirable to fly the bird "out of the hood" at quarry, but even if the falconer never intends to hunt in this way, hooding can still be a great help when working with these big birds.

Some excellent eagle hoods are available from European and North American sources. Some of these are based on the Dutch pattern; others are of Anglo-Indian design. Kirghiz and Kazakh hoods from central Asia work very well and no small number of European eagle enthusiasts favor Asian hoods. Unlike Anglo-Indian or Dutch-style hoods, Kirghiz and Kazakh hoods have no braces and rely on their shape and fit to keep them in place.

Lures

Lures for eagles can be made up by simply stuffing pelts with suitable material. However, if one can use whole carcasses or skins with the heads left on, these will make better training lures. These "natural" lures will withstand a lot of punishment and the bird can actually be rewarded from the deceased animal's head.

Housing

Experienced falconers will have their own ideas about what constitutes the perfect eagle housing arrangement. Many of the housing options one sees are simply variations on a basic theme, but some are quite elaborate affairs. Generally, from a safety point of view, the more basic one can keep things, the better. The more intricate and complicated the design, the more chance there is of an accident.

A commonly used housing arrangement is simply a large, open-fronted lean-to, with one perch positioned underneath and another outside. A longish leash allows the eagle to choose where it sits. Very important, however, is that the leash is not so long that the eagle can get it tangled around the outer perch. Also, the roof of the lean-to will need to be high enough and the leash short enough, to prevent the eagle getting on to the front edge of the structure. The floor of the lean-to is covered with a generous layer of smooth gravel.

A less desirable housing option is the use of a smallish A-frame-type shelter that has a taut wire running out from it to a perch some distance away. The leash is attached to this wire by a metal ring, thus allowing the eagle to fly to and from its shelter as it pleases. This arrangement has definite disadvantages. For example, until familiar with the restrictions imposed on it, the eagle may attempt to fly around the side of the shelter.

At the Renaissance Falkenhof in Austria, eagles are housed in a rather grand manner. A row of spacious alcoves, set in a courtyard wall, have been modified to shelter individual birds. Each alcove has a low block positioned quite near to its front edge, with an alternative outside perch (in the form of a large rock) a little distance away. Around the outer perch is an area of deepish, smooth gravel; into this is sunk an eagle bath. As with a more modest lean-to arrangement, a longish leash allows the occupying eagle to choose where it sits. In front of the eagle alcoves is an area of grass, into which individual blocks or perches can be driven when daily cleaning chores require any eagles to be temporarily moved. This small lawn also puts a sensible distance between eagles and the visitors who are invited to walk the path that surrounds the set-up. This alcove arrangement, which houses both flying display birds, such as imperial eagles and golden eagles that are used for hunting, has proven very satisfactory.

The idea of providing an alternative perch for a tethered eagle may strike some falconers as rather risky. On the surface it does seem that the bird would be certain to damage its plumage on the outer perching place. The worry, and a quite natural one, is that an eagle bating on the floor next to this perch will strike it with its wings. Yet in practice this type of thing should not prove to be a problem. A golden eagle is highly intelligent and if accustomed to a double perch arrangement can be kept in perfect feather condition. If the bird feels the urge to move it goes forwards on to the outer perch, rather than simply bate into the blue. It is important that the outside perch be stout, broad and topped with rubber (even the Renaissance Falkenhof rocks are topped with rubber). This perch must be tall enough to make it tempting, it should be no lower than the inside perch. Generally eagles like an alternative perching place and the perch they choose will be influenced by the weather, time of day and even the mood they are in. A bird that has been sitting out all day will invariably seek the security of its inside roosting place when darkness falls.

Some falconers prefer to keep their eagles tethered to one perch under a lean-to. This arrangement normally sees the shelter large enough to prevent the bird being exposed to the open sky at all. The floor covering is deep sand and this the bird bates on to. This is a tried and tested arrangement for all manner of hunting hawks. Nevertheless, the disadvantage is that the bird is restricted to one perch with one surface. With a double perch set-up the eagle can be offered flat and round surfaces and this can only be seen as beneficial. Whether one or two perches are provided will depend very much upon the bird's background. If the bird is accustomed to having an alternative perch then it may very well not settle if tied to a single perch. At the same time, if the eagle has never been given a second perch then it might possibly damage its plumage if placed in a double perch housing arrangement.

The housing arrangement designed by one falconer seemed quite successful. Again it was a standard lean-to set-up but instead of having a second perch for the bird he built a small wooden wall in front of the shelter (this was not intended as a perch). Following a bate, the bird found its field of vision blocked by this wall and so immediately went back on to its single perch, from where its view was uninterupted. The idea was to make the ground as uninviting for the bird as possible. The set-up was modified in one other way. An arcing strip of flat rubber was laid for the bird to bate on to. This was designed as a soft clean landing pad for the bird's precious feet.

No matter how good the eagle's housing is, I am a very firm believer in getting the bird out of its shelter as much as possible. There is no reason why the bird should not spend a large portion of the day on a lawn perch. The bird's position should be regularly altered so that it can benefit from a change of scene. Birds that are not familiar with being out on a lawn perch can actually become very restless when they find themselves open and exposed. It is vitally important therefore to have the bird used to both arrangements.

After looking at more normal housing options I would like to mention a final possibility, and that is keeping the bird loose in a spacious mews. I have successfully used wooden buildings with several species. In each case the mews contained a single vertical barred window allowing the bird to see out. This type of housing is nothing new and has been described by several authors. That said, I have not kept hunting sharp golden eagles loose in this fashion. I have seen it done but in both cases the building was completely enclosed except for the roof. If to keep an eagle loose means it has to be robbed of all visual stimulation then tethering would be my personal choice.

When constructing any housing arrangement care must be taken to build using timber that is sufficiently stout. Although I have used the term "lean-to" it is not my intention to suggest some quickly thrown together eagle houses.

By necessity an eagle's shelter (or mews) will need to be large and, of course, the larger the structure the stronger it will have to be. Special attention should be paid to roofs which have to cope with snow fall.

Transport

Golden eagles are big birds and taking a slap-dash attitude towards transporting them can spell trouble not only for the birds themselves, but also for the other occupants of any vehicle they are being transported in. It does not take much imagination to visualize what might happen if an eagle started thrashing about in the back of an estate car.

The safest and certainly the least worrying way of transporting eagles is to use specifically made boxes. Generally speaking, I prefer to keep transport boxes fairly small, although I always allow enough room for the eagle to turn round. With these points in mind, a box measuring (inside) 55 centimeters by 55 centimeters by 80 centimeters will be found ideal for either a male or female eagle. The interior of the box should be completely smooth, painted with gloss paint or finished preferably in melamine. This reduces any risk of damaged feathers and also makes cleaning the box out much easier.

Ventilation is provided by four large air holes in the front of the box and one each side high up at the rear. This type of transport box contains no perch at all: the eagle simply sits on the floor. A snugly fitting piece of carpet gives the bird something to grip. Before each journey, the carpet is covered with a sheet of paper. The purpose of this is to protect tail tips and keep things clean. With this design, I have yet to experience any problems with damaged feathers.

4 Training

In the areas where golden eagle falconry has its origins, wild-taken passage eagles have always been highly valued. Historically, the early taming and training of these birds revolved very much around extreme weight control and depriving the subject of sleep. The principle was to reduce the bird both mentally and physically until it became more biddable.

Keeping newly trapped birds awake or "watching" them was a practice once employed in Europe with goshawks. The goshawk was simply kept unhooded on the falconer's hand until it ceased bating and accepted the fist as a perch. Tired and exhausted, the bird eventually had to sleep. The taming of these hawks relied on continually carrying them and exposing them to all manner of things. Day after day the carrying continued until the terrified bird slowly and grudgingly became accustomed to its new environment.

In Asia, the golden eagle was subjected to a rather different type of treatment. First, a hood was always employed and secondly, the wearing-down process might involve the use of a moving perch. The hooded eagle was placed on a suspended pole-type perch that was kept constantly in motion. Not very demanding on the falconer or anyone else asked to keep the perch swinging, but very draining for the desperately tired eagle. Several nineteenth-century writers mention such techniques and some give graphic accounts of how individual eagles were reduced in condition to a point where they could no longer achieve flight. Initial training sessions would simply see the bird enticed to half-run, half-fly after a lure.

Very little information of any real practical value can be gleaned from the older accounts. Nevertheless, the modern European and North American falconer would be well advised to adopt the Asian practice of hooding. In this respect, the newly acquired passage or fully feathered, captive-bred bird should be handled more as if it were a falcon. The hood is introduced at the very start of the taming process and used continually throughout training. The manning or taming of an eagle is basically no different from that of any other hunting bird. Success is achieved by a slow, steady approach and does not involve carrying the bird for lengthy periods or the use of other "force tactics." The modern falconer wins his charge over using food. He does not try to bludgeon the bird into submission.

The Hand-reared Eyas

The passage, or fully developed aviary-bred eagle, is tamed by learning to associate the falconer with food. Taming and early training sessions are kept short, as the hungry, feeding eagle slowly comes to accept and trust the falconer. With the hand-reared eyas, the situation is completely different. As it grows, the nestling eagle is kept constantly around the falconer and other people and is kept where it can see other birds. It is well fed and exposed to as much activity as possible. All of the things that the passage or aviary-reared bird will have to be introduced carefully to, the eyas simply learns to accept as it develops. Noisy vehicles, groups of people, dogs and horses: all of these things and more can be introduced to the eyas long before it can fly.

Perhaps at this stage something should be said on group rearing. Due to the sibling aggression witnessed in wild-living eagles, precautions need to be taken when one is rearing more than one bird. While it is important for the young eagle to see other birds during its early days, it would be wise to keep it physically separated from other young eagles until all are fairly well developed. Once partially feathered and the risk period is over, two or even three young eagles can normally be allowed to spend time together—this of course, under the closest supervision.

When rearing his eagle, the falconer may be tempted to keep his prized possession away from a lot of activity, feeling it might be more desirable to rear the bird in total privacy, but jealously guarding his charge in this way will do far more harm than good. Even when fully developed, the eagle should be housed where it can observe busy scenes. Mental stimulation is vitally important for these intelligent raptors, and, if kept isolated, the hand-reared eagle's temperament will suffer.

With a totally tame, hand-reared eagle, the rearing should flow into basic training, and, as a large, fairly well-feathered youngster, the eagle can be slowly introduced to the idea of wearing jesses, being carried on the fist, tied to a block and being hooded. These things can easily be accomplished with a bird that is quite advanced, but has not yet reached the flight stage. If the basics are left until the very last moment, then there is a risk that the now very active and flight-capable eagle will damage its plumage, which will still be "in the blood."

Obviously, a little common sense is required with early training. If the bird is tied to a block, then it must be a very low one (it is well worth constructing an especially low beginner's block). It must be positioned on smooth grass and well away from anything the eagle might come into contact with. Rather than have the grass really short, a few centimeters growth makes the area around the block a little softer. At night, the young eagle is returned to the mews, where it is kept entirely free. It should not be tethered under any kind of lean-to structure until it is slightly older and, of course, totally accepts being restrained. If introduced earlier rather than later, an eagle will settle down very quickly to the idea of being tied.

Something that requires special mention is hooding. With hand-reared hawks and falcons, it has become standard practice to begin hooding very early on. In principle, hand-reared golden eagles are no exception; however, hooding need not begin terribly early and making a start as soon as the eagle's head has that "finished" look about it will be quite soon enough. Success with hooding relies on introducing the hood gradually and with feeling. To begin with, the pupil is hooded for just a moment or two (the hood being left in its open position). Day by day, the hood is left on for longer periods, all the time the eagle getting more accustomed to the procedure. Of paramount importance is that the hood employed is light in weight and comfortable for the bird. True Dutch hoods are not suitable, but some of the modern eagle hoods that are loosely based on the traditional Dutch pattern are excellent. Braceless Kirghiz and Kazakh hoods are not suitable for early hood-training sessions.

When hooding is being attempted late (after the bird is hard-penned), the hand-reared eagle may react in a number of ways; and, here, the individual bird's temperament plays a part. One bird might be slowly won over, while another may never become really well made to the hood. Such a bird might allow itself to be hooded, but then be restless under the hood. It is worth noting that, just because a young eagle allows a hood to be placed over its head, it does not automatically follow that it accepts hooding full stop. So that the relationship between eagle and trainer does not suffer, I strongly recommend early hood training.

Another aspect of training that needs to be covered before the eagle is hard-penned is the introduction of lure carcasses. As soon as the young bird is able to pull at food for itself, it should be encouraged to feed from large, whole carcasses, these being opened up slightly to allow easy access. This is most important, for it orientates the eyas to "fur" as a source of food and therefore does away with a more formal introduction at a later stage.

If brought along in this way, a hand-reared eyas will have been taught most of the basics long before its aviary-reared counterpart is even removed from the breeding enclosure.

Weight Control

Basic flight training commences as soon as the young eagle is hard-penned. Up to this point, the eagle's food will not have been rationed or its weight monitored in any great detail. This now changes. If the eagle is to respond to training and react when the falconer wishes it to, rather than when it pleases, its food intake must be governed. Weight control is often depicted as being something of a nightmare with eagles (revolving around long periods of starvation), but this is simply not the case. Any experienced falconer who has worked with large buteos should be able to adjust to an eagle's requirements without too much difficulty. What might surprise the new eagle owner is just how much food a young bird being flown hard actually needs. A young golden eagle continues to develop long after it is fully fledged and this must be accounted for. If not, there is a very good chance the bird will end up too "low"; and it is not at all unusual to see a young eagle taken afield in too low a condition.

With a young eagle, the inexperienced owner often comes unstuck by interpreting genuine bad luck on the bird's part as a lack of enthusiasm for the chase. To combat this, the bird's weight is brought down and down some more and soon the falconer will know all about lack of enthusiasm, for his charge will have interest in nothing. It often takes a skilled eye to know whether a young eagle is really trying or not. Naturally, in the case of a blatant refusal, the matter is clear-cut. However, when active and agile quarries are actually being pursued (unsuccessfully), assessing the bird's performance accurately requires experience. Even when the bird is judged to be a fraction "high," the seasoned eagle falconer will tread very carefully when adjusting a young bird's weight. Older birds (second year onwards) require less food and will fly heavier than in their first year.

Basic Management

In this section, I would like to look at several rather rudimentary aspects of eagle management, beginning with the picking-up and carrying of the bird. It is fairly common procedure to pick up trained hunting birds from their blocks or perches with a hand-held tidbit. With hand-reared eagles, this is not only unnecessary, but also inadvisable. As training begins and the eagle's weight is monitored, its interest in food naturally becomes stronger. As it does, the falconer will need to be increasingly careful regarding how and where he feeds his charge. In the area where it is normally housed, the eagle's reaction to food will be very strong; and, if fed on the fist at its block, its manners will leave a lot to be desired. Because of this, tid-bitting

36

at the block should be avoided. The eagle must not come to associate its trainer's approach automatically with food. When the eagle needs to be fed on the fist at home, it is well worth moving it to another area beforehand.

To begin with, the carrying of an eagle can cause the person more used to the weight of a goshawk-sized bird a few problems. Here, I would suggest keeping the eagle close to one's body and periodically using the ungloved hand to support the bird-carrying arm. With this position, one needs to be careful with hooded eagles. If the eagle shakes its head, the braces of an Anglo-Indian-type hood will be at just the right height to give the falconer a nasty whip across his face. Successful carrying relies a great deal on getting the eagle balanced and comfortable. This is especially true in the case of a hooded bird, which relies very much on its trainer for comfort. With time and practice, the eagle's weight will become less of an issue (large females excepted!) and falconer and bird will become more like one, rather than two parties struggling against each other. Out in the field, this type of unity is terribly important, for if one cannot move freely, hawking opportunities will be lost.

Related to the topic of carrying an eagle is that of dealing with a restless bird. The eagle that already seems heavy to carry can become an unbearable burden for its owner if it starts to bate from the fist. It is not just the eagle's weight, but there is also the powerful beating of its huge wings and the need to keep these from making contact with the ground or other objects. Even totally tame, hand-reared eagles will bate (even when hooded) and so the falconer will need to be able to deal with this. First, I would recommend trying to avoid the odd bate. This can be achieved by placing the ungloved hand against the eagle's chest as it prepares to bate. In effect, one is holding the bird in position. This can be very effective when a restless bird seems likely to spoil a developing hunting opportunity by bating at the crucial moment. Unless over-"petted" or manhandled as a youngster, the eagle will not resent this restraining tactic. That said, if overdone, the eagle will certainly build resentment and so the falconer should only view holding his eagle back as a way of forestalling an inconvenient bate. This is not a technique designed to prevent bating altogether.

Due to the eagle's weight, it is very tempting to lift it back to the fist (hand under chest) while it is actually bating. This midbate interruption will definitely reduce arm and hand strain, but will often leave a restless bird still unsettled. It is sometimes far better to let the bird bate heartily before lifting it back to the fist. When this is done, it will normally settle down.

Bating frequently occurs when eagles are keyed up for the hunt or a training session. When hawking with an active, restless bird, it is often prudent to allow it to fly before commencing the hunt. A short flight will enable the eagle to release some of its pent-up energy and calm it mentally. If not permitted to stretch its wings, the eagle might well remain fidgety, making its owner's life hard and ruining flight opportunities.

For dealing with an eagle's basic management requirements at home, the falconer will follow the same sort of routine as for other hunting birds. Perches are kept clean, the housing arrangement itself dry and the eagle given daily access to fresh water. Talons, feet and feathers must be checked regularly. Sharp talons are a must and so often make the difference between quarry being taken or not. Looking at an eagle's huge feet, one might think that slightly blunt talons would not affect its game-catching ability too seriously. But sharp talons are as important to an eagle as they are to any hawk or buteo. With large quarry, the sharper the talons, the more easily they can be driven into the victim; and the deeper they go, the better the hold. With small, more elusive quarry, just getting to grips with the intended victim can prove a problem. A foot equipped with razor-sharp talons making a snatch at a dodging, jinking target is far more likely to obtain a penetrating grip than a foot armed with blunt talons.

Blunt talons must be sharpened manually with a small file and for this, assistance is really required. The eagle is hooded, and, as it sits on the fist, its weaponry is attended to. Of primary concern are the main front-inside and rear talons. Sharpening in this way can certainly make a big difference, but one never seems to get a finish quite as good as the natural version. Because of this, every effort should be made to keep the talons sharp in the first place. If the eagle's talons are continually being rounded off, then its owner must search for the cause. Often, the eagle's housing set-up will be at fault. For example, if the eagle is constantly bating onto the ground rather than "hopping" to an alternative perch, its talons will naturally suffer. In such a case, the actual location of the lean-to shelter might be causing the problem. If the eagle is convinced that to the left or right of it there is something worth investigating (noise, activity, possible food!), it will not move forwards onto its outer perch or block, but busy itself attempting to get around whichever "blind side" it finds interesting.

I have never had any serious foot problems with golden eagles, but that does not prevent me worrying about the possibility. The slightest cut or nick could develop into something if it goes unnoticed, and, because of this, I am quite fussy about keeping an eagle's feet clean. If, after a day's hawking, the eagle ends up with bloody or particularly dirty feet, I wash them using a small, hand-held brush. The procedure is quite simple. The eagle is hooded and its feet are cleaned as it sits on the fist. One can manage this alone, and, if the job is done quickly, the eagle should sit quietly throughout. If the eagle has been flown to aggressive quarries, checking and cleaning its feet (and legs) is vitally important.

Finally, under this heading of basic management, I would like to look at the business of traveling with eagles. For hunting, or even training trips, a transport box is fairly essential. A suitable box has already been described in the equipment chapter, but the eagle will need to be carefully introduced to it if such a transport aid is to be of any use at all. Unless the eagle arrives at its destination settled and happy, there will be little chance of any hunting, or even training, being done. To begin with, the eagle is placed inside the box for just a minute or two. Each day, this period is extended until short drives can be undertaken without the bird becoming distressed. During this period, I tend to wet primary and tail tips with cold water before putting the eagle in its box. A wet feather tip is far less likely to suffer damage than a dry one.

The procedure for placing an eagle in its transport box is fairly straightforward. The bird is simply backed into the box as it sits on the fist. As this is being done, the falconer uses his body to block the eagle's view, this prevents it bating. In addition, if the ungloved hand is placed over the eagle's head (actually just touching it), this too will help guide the subject into the box without incident. Once the eagle is inside, the fist is wriggled from under the bird's feet and withdrawn (on feeling the floor of the box, the eagle will let go of the glove). The occupant is removed by taking hold of its jesses and easing it onto the fist as it is drawn out of the box. If, when the door is opened, the eagle is facing backwards, then no attempt should be made to remove it; this may result in the bird struggling to remain in the box. The best course of action is to shut the door and wait for a moment or two. This pause will frequently see the eagle turn around of its own accord. If it does not alter its position, then the gloved hand can be used to try to initiate the turning process. No food is used to tempt the bird into or out of the box. No leash is attached to the jesses (in case the bird becomes entangled) and no hood is employed.

When transporting eagles, every effort should be made to ensure that the bird's mutes do not foul the inside of the box, for this in turn will lead to soiled plumage. If a long journey is being contemplated, the falconer must plan ahead and calculate the eagle's weight so that it can be transported "empty." Also, the vehicle should be halted every two hours and the eagle removed from its box. With experience, eagles get used to this regular traveling break and very quickly put it to good use.

Flying to the Fist

Some falconers prefer not to call golden eagles to the fist, yet, in my experience, these are in the minority. Some, wishing for less direct contact with these big birds, have looked for alternatives. The use of a garnished T-perch is a possibility, although here I have no personal experience. I have even seen birds called to tidbits thrown down for them on the ground.

Flying golden eagles to the fist should not be viewed as a dangerous practice. It can be accomplished without any problems at all as long as the falconer follows one or two guidelines. The first and most important rule is not to openly remove food from the bird as it sits on the fist (or anywhere else, for that matter). The bird should be called to the glove for small tidbits and allowed to consume these completely and without interference. If the bird is robbed on the fist, sooner or later it will take steps to prevent the robbery and this, as can be imagined, can be a serious business for its foolish handler. The bird that cannot be trusted with bare hands makes life very difficult when one is attempting to secure its jesses after it has landed on the fist. That the jesses are secured is vitally important with young hand-reared birds, for the close proximity of the falconer to them and their food can result in them becoming protective. If the jesses are not taken hold of, the eagle may well try to grab the falconer's upper arm.

The second point I would like to mention also concerns the bird's behavior on the fist. If a large amount of food is displayed on the fist, there is a greater chance of the bird becoming protective of the meal. When one wishes to call the bird in for a largish reward, the majority of it should be concealed in the fist, with only a small amount protruding. The bird will, of course, be allowed to eat whatever the fist contains.

Young hand-reared golden eagles will come huge distances to the fist for the tiniest reward. Sometimes, however, especially under hunting conditions when the bird's attention is focused on more interesting matters, some encouragement may be required. At such times, more food can be displayed on the fist (in addition to the tidbit), but as soon as the bird begins its approach, this should be discreetly removed and placed in the hawking bag. This will not result in resentment as long as the bird does not witness the trickery. As always, the bird lands to receive its normal and expected tidbit.

The thing to always remember when calling eagles to the fist is to behave calmly and move steadily. For example, if, when the bird lands, the falconer finds it difficult to secure both jesses in the conventional way, he should take hold of them in any way possible (the jess on the leg nearest the falconer is often awkward to secure in the proper manner). As the bird relaxes, its jesses can be repositioned. He should not allow himself to become flustered, fumbling to do things the proper way. This is especially important with abused birds that half-expect to be robbed. Something to avoid at all costs is touching the bird as it eats. If the bird's stance on the fist seems "untidy," the falconer should never attempt to correct this manually; the bird will feel the falconer is a threat to its food and react accordingly. On the subject of avoiding problems, if a tidbit drops from the fist to the ground and the bird follows it down (before its jesses are secured), the best plan is to move right away and call the bird back to another tidbit. If one remains towering above the bird, it will again feel its food is threatened.

With the idea of trying to build a personal and individual bond with his bird, the falconer may be tempted to fly it alone, never enlisting the help of an assistant. This is not a good idea with hand-reared eagles. Rather than have the bird bond to and trust only one individual, it makes far better sense to have it accept people in general. With this in mind, if the falconer has an experienced colleague, this person should also fly the eagle during flying-to-the-fist sessions. If the young eagle is flown by two or even three people, its manners will be better for it later, providing, that is, no inexperienced hand has been allowed to dabble.

Lure Training

Once the bird is responding well, it is quite easy for the falconer to concentrate too much on flying-to-the-fist exercises. Here, he may be encouraged by his pupil's enthusiasm. Young eagles love nothing more than flying into the glove for tasty tidbits and their attentiveness is naturally pleasing. However, time must be spent on lure work. The young eagle's early introduction to whole carcasses should not now be wasted and more advanced training and field preparation will revolve around reinforcing the bird's liking for "fur."

I cannot emphasize strongly enough how vital the right kind of lure work is with young, totally inexperienced eagles. Not only does the lure prepare the bird for flying at real quarry, but it also teaches (if gone about correctly) the importance of securing this quarry by the head. In addition, it takes the focus off the falconer as a source of easy meals, helping the bird to become more independent and mature in its thinking. During training, the eagle should continue to be flown to the fist, but lure work is where things are really achieved.

The importance of obtaining a head grip is taught in two ways. First, the eagle is only fed at the head end of the lure. If a fox or roe deer pelt with the head attached is being used, then the head should have a slight incision made in it, in the under jaw area. Secondly, if the eagle takes hold of the lure anywhere else, it is given a rather rough ride. By this I do not mean that bird and lure are simply dragged off at full speed in a straight line. One wants to help the pupil understand where it is going wrong, not simply punish it! The training lure itself will be (or should be) a large object with the lure-line attached at the front. This means that if the lure is taken from behind, the lure-line can be used not only to pull and tug it left and right, but also to bring the front end (or actual head if a carcass or headed pelt is being used) off the ground. Working the lure in this way should soon teach the bird that its "victim" can only be brought under control and food obtained when its front end is secured. Not that all movement of the lure should cease once it has been taken correctly. This would then give the impression that, once held by the head, prey is totally passive. Whenever a young eagle is called to the lure, a simulated struggle is essential even when the lure is taken perfectly. Tidbits on the fist and immobile lures represent easy options and easy options are things young eagles should be steered away from. Subjecting the bird to a simulated struggle with wild quarry also has another purpose. Hand-reared eagles can become very possessive over lures. If allowed simply to land and feed, the eagle's attention will be on the falconer as he approaches and this approach may well be resented. Each step sees the bird's protective stance becoming more exaggerated. With hackles raised and wings spread, the emotionally aroused creature will do its best to intimidate the offending human. On the other hand, if put through a vigorous mock battle with prey, all the eagle's attention will be directed towards subduing its victim. When the falconer approaches now, he will be almost ignored.

A golden eagle's ability to intimidate is not something to be made light of. Everything about the bird's behavior warns the falconer to keep well away, and, aware of the physical damage the bird is capable of inflicting, the warning is frequently heeded. The result is that the falconer dithers on the sidelines while the bird slowly becomes the more dominant partner. If the bird really succeeds in terrifying and dominating its trainer, then all will be lost. Things will go from bad to worse and soon the human will find himself in possession of an eagle he can do nothing with. This is where so many would-be eagle flyers go wrong with hand-reared birds. They assume a passive, gentle role, when really they should be acting more confidently. Positive thinking is the key. It should be remembered that any difficulties experienced during early training can be overcome if the trainer adopts the right mental attitude. The pupil that was awkward and insolent will become manageable and obliging.

Without the right help and guidance, negotiating one's way over early hurdles can be a formidable challenge. Even those who consider themselves quite experienced with smaller hunting birds can find the training of a hand-reared eagle a worrying business. Worried was how I found an old German friend a few years ago. Having heard that he had acquired his first golden eagle and keen to see how the bird was coming along, I paid him a visit. I had been told that the eagle, a female, was an extremely handsome individual. This she was, but attractive is not how one could have described her behavior. It soon became clear that this large female eagle was calling the tune and had her owner almost exactly where she wanted him. It would be incorrect to say that he was truly frightened: this he was not. However, there were certain aspects of the bird's management that were obviously causing him great concern. Before going any further, I should mention that I had an English guest with me who had seen an older, really well-mannered, hand-reared eagle being flown. That said, he had not witnessed the little problems one can encounter during early training sessions.

Our host inquired if we would like to assist with a spot of training and this we, or should I say I, agreed to do. First thing on the agenda was a little fist-to-fist flying and it was with this that I first got an inkling that something was amiss. In the stage she was at, the bird should have been quite manageable. But, although not aggressive to the point of being dangerous, everything about her indicated that she had not really settled into training at all. Perhaps it was her size. Perhaps it was the fact that she came into the fist like a charging buffalo. But her first flight saw our English spectator taking a few steps back from his already distant position.

Finishing off with a lure flight was suggested, this apparently being the normal conclusion to every training session. The word "conclusion" sounded a little strange, but I was soon to be enlightened. Off her owner went, dragging the lure behind him and I let the eagle go. A nice fast flight followed and the bird quickly had her prize. As the bird sat on the motionless lure, she mantled wildly and, with crest feathers erect and head back, her true size was magnified many times. It was now that our host's problem came to the surface. Faced with this impressive display, he seemed rooted to the spot. There was an embarrassed silence as we waited and watched. The poor fellow was obviously extremely nervous about approaching his charge. He now informed us that we would have to wait until she calmed down! The eagle was in control of the situation and knew it. As far as she was concerned, training was over.

That my old friend needed a little help was all too clear and this he shortly asked for. Without any hesitation, I suggested that he employ the "mock battle tactic" following each and every lure flight and rather than keep away from the bird, he should in fact go in to her and get her used to his approach. This way, she would slowly stop regarding him as a threat as he hovered in the shadows. Right there and then he put my advice into practice and was amazed to find the bird immediately more amenable. It is worth adding that this eagle went on to be rewarding to fly and very effective against wild quarry.

It is essential to feel comfortable about making in to any young eagle guarding a lure. Without confidence, it will be impossible to take the eagle up from the lure in the proper manner, or indeed help it find and feed from the correct end of the thing. This goes back to teaching the importance of securing a head-hold. During early training sessions, a hand-reared eagle can get so worked up, turning this way and that in an effort to protect its prize, that the falconer may need to almost push the lure's head under the eagle's beak so that it can feed.

Removing a young eagle from lures requires a great deal of care. Here, one needs to operate (as with flying to the fist) without creating an atmosphere of suspicion and distrust. To this end, the eagle should be approached from the front in a positive and direct manner. Crouching down, the falconer offers the eagle a piece of substitute meat held tightly in his gloved hand; this should be pressed against the lure where the eagle was feeding. The bird will now take hold of the fist and begin to eat. As it does this, it is lifted slightly and a hawking bag is eased over the area where the eagle was initially feeding. Now, making sure the bird's attention is still on the meat in his fist, the falconer moves over and away from the lure, using his body to shield it from the bird. It is during this procedure that the jesses are taken hold of. An assistant now moves in and quickly and discreetly hides the lure (that is, places it in a rucksack). The whole procedure should run smoothly and without incident. If the eagle is forced off the lure or bates to get back to it, then the falconer and his field helper are failing in their jobs.

One can find descriptions of eagles being taken up off lures (or quarry) in other ways. One procedure involves the falconer approaching from behind and attempting to grasp the jesses before the bird is offered any reward at all. The immediate concern seems to be controlling the eagle's movements. However, groping around in this way will inevitably put the bird on its guard. Even if the maneuver is successful, the falconer will find himself in a very awkward position. How is the bird to be offered a reward if the gloved hand is occupied with holding the jesses? When taken up in the correct manner, the professionally trained and handled eagle is controlled by the skillful use of a hand-held reward. It is not pulled off lures or quarry with its jesses.

Flying in Woodland

An aspect of eagle training often overlooked is that of flying in woodland. Woodland work is absolutely vital, for it gives the young eagle maneuverability and also gears it for actually hunting through tree cover. If conditioned to fly in woodland from an early age, golden eagles can demonstrate breath-taking ability in this environment.

To begin with, the young bird will be encouraged to go into individual trees from which it will be recalled to the fist. This may sound rather rudimentary stuff, but young eagles, new to the flying game, can be extremely clumsy. Simply landing in trees requires practice. Until the bird is able to perform this basic task, very little can be done in terms of true woodland work. Although eventually the eagle will be capable of functioning under surprisingly tight conditions, initial training will be conducted in more open woodland. This training takes two forms: following-on from tree to tree and responding to the fist and lure work. Getting the youngster to follow-on is not a difficult task. It is bonded to its trainer and associates him with positive things. Initially, the bird will be periodically called in to the fist as it shadows its trainer through the trees. As things progress, however, the bird will need to be rewarded less, and, if it is lagging behind, a simple wave of the hand should bring it on. Indeed, when hawking, tidbitting is to be avoided, as it takes the bird's mind off hunting.

Lure work in woodland should be as varied as the terrain and tree density allows. Where hollows and banks occur, these can be put to good use and any natural feature should be exploited in an effort to simulate hunting situations.

Whether lures are being pulled out in the open or among trees one wants them to appear "alive." They can be hidden in clumps of cover and be made to suddenly materialize ahead of the eagle. They should be pulled erratically and pulled quickly! On no account should the bird be allowed to take hold of a stationary lure. If the eagle lands near the lure, this should then be pulled away. If the bird pursues, all well and good; if not, the lure should be concealed and preparations made for another flight.

Lure flights in woodland settings can either be very simple or made stimulating and demanding for man and bird. As the eagle's skill develops, it should not be allowed to stagnate and the falconer should be constantly thinking of ways to vary training sessions.

Woodland work does not just revolve around the bird being called from trees. Flights from the fist to lures being pulled by helpers are certainly worthwhile and these flights are some of the more interesting ones. They are introduced as simple, straightforward pursuits, with the eagle being hooded off to a lure immediately visible and no great distance away. But as the eagle becomes more familiar with the routine, these mock hunts should be made increasingly more difficult. As more obstacles (increased tree density, cover and so on) are placed between the bird and lure, flights can be extremely lengthy and somewhat indirect. A typical flight at a fairly advanced stage of training might see the lure itself visible throughout the chase or periodically hidden as the lure-man weaves his way at full speed through the forest. Really, the bird is pursuing by sight and sound. Repetition has geared it to fly at almost the slightest disturbance and it is not uncommon for the extremely keyed-up eagle to leave the glove before actually seeing anything. In such instances, the bird may touch down for a second on a tree limb before locking onto the lure and commencing the hunt proper. There is nothing "flappy" or lethargic about the bird's pursuit style; it is flying in an eager, almost frenzied fashion. Its eagerness may see it snapping off twigs and breaking fine, brittle branches as it desperately tries to close with the lure.

These woodland lure flights require a degree of preplanning and much of this planning will be done by the lure-man. He, of course, will require not only an intimate knowledge of the bird and its level of training, but also of the terrain he is intending to run over. Fine calculations are impossible with this type of thing, but the lure-man will need to have a rough picture in his mind of exactly how and where he will pull the lure. He should also be able to judge approximately where eagle and lure will meet. On entering the woods, the plan of action will be explained to the falconer, who will then wait with the hooded eagle until his companion is in position. It is now that the lure-man's work really begins. Pulling the lure would be strenuous enough on flat, even ground, but weaving through trees and dodging other obstacles makes the task a draining one for even the most physically fit. Yet there is more. All of this is conducted at speed, across rough ground dragging a lure that will be catching against and bouncing off obstructions. At the same time, the poor man has to keep his eye on the pursuing eagle.

Woodland lure flights need not always begin actually within the cover of the trees. Flights can be arranged in such a way that they start out in the open and finish in cover. Fine flights can be obtained where open ground contains an area of woodland. The falconer waits with his hooded eagle in the open, while, some distance away, an assistant readies himself with a lure. At a signal from the falconer, the lure-man heads for the trees at his best pace. The eagle is unhooded and slipped. What one is aiming for with this type of flight is for the eagle to pursue the lure deep into the trees, and, with a little practice, this is not difficult to achieve. Everything revolves around timing. The lure-man should not enter the trees too far ahead of the bird. By the same token, he cannot afford to leave things too late; if he does, the eagle will take the lure either in the open or on the woodland edge.

Fitness Training

If a golden eagle is going to do well in direct pursuit-type flights from the fist, it will need to be fit. Standard lure training will develop the eagle's physical condition, but to bring that condition to a pitch of fine hunting fitness, I would recommend employing mechanical aid. If at all possible, the eagle should be flown to lures pulled across country by either a jeep or motorcycle. Of course, this type of thing takes some arranging, but if the necessary help is on hand and the mechanical ingredient available, it really is well worth trying.

An essential requirement for motorized lure work is an extensive area of flat, open ground. Rough terrain is out of the question due to the fact that the training area will need to be traversed at speed.

Given suitable ground and a team of three people, the actual technique is very much the same whether one is using a cross-country motorcycle or jeep. To keep things straightforward, I will outline the procedure with just one of these: the motorcycle. The falconer waits with the hooded eagle until his two assistants (on the motorcycle) are in a suitable position. Just how far away they are from the falconer will depend on the bird's experience and level of fitness. With the falconer ready, they pull away dragging the lure on a long line behind them. The eagle is unhooded and slipped. At this stage, the pillion rider on the rear of the motorcycle is very much in control of things. His job now is to instruct the driver to either slow down or speed up, depending on the eagle's distance from the lure. The bird's interest must be held if a long flight is to be achieved. In time, these training flights can become very long, and, as the bird gets to know the routine and gains fitness, the team's job is made more difficult. The real skill is in judging the eagle's performance as it is actually flying. A simple enough task for the observer standing on the sidelines, but not so easy for the person traveling at speed on the back of a motorcycle.

When the pillion rider feels the eagle has worked hard enough, he will allow the lure to be taken (while it is still in motion). The actual lure-line is dropped immediately to prevent the bird suffering an injury. The motorcycle is now halted, enabling the pillion rider-*cum*-lure-man to return quickly to the eagle. Once there, he will tug the lure a little to simulate, as always, a struggle. While this is being done, the motorcyclist heads off to pick up the falconer, who may be a considerable distance away. After the bird has been allowed a short rest and the team has once again composed themselves, the operation is repeated in the opposite direction.

As an alternative to using a motorcycle or jeep, the services of a horse might be called upon. Two of my falconry colleagues actually prefer to use a horse, stating that it makes the behavior of the lure less predictable, this due to the movement of the horse. When a horse is employed, only a two-man team is required as the rider also acts as lure-man.

Naturally, the horse's value does not start and finish with the pulling of lures. There is no reason why the European or North American falconer (landscape and quarry permitting) should not adopt the central Asian practice of hunting from the saddle. Here, a word of caution. Although the eagle and horse partnership is an ancient one, great care should be exercised when introducing the two as mistakes made here can be serious. It should not be assumed that the horse will simply accept a bird the size of a golden eagle flying to and from its rider. Even with lure work, nothing should be taken for granted and it is this need for caution (and horsemanship) that would perhaps sway many falconers more toward a jeep or motorcycle as a lure-training aid.

Whether using a horse or a vehicle, this type of training must be conducted with feeling. If it is gone about sensibly, the results can be most impressive, however it should not be overdone and, the bird's reactions must always be carefully noted. Specialized fitness training should never be seen as an answer in itself, for this it is not. It should be included as part of the overall training program and not concentrated on alone.

Soaring

Under the right conditions, golden eagles can be highly aerial and soaring flights with these birds can be fascinating and dramatic. Some eagle owners concentrate solely on soaring, never flying off the glove and never hawking in locations where soaring flights are difficult to achieve. This is specialized work, but even the falconer who hunts primarily from the fist will occasionally find himself in situations where the bird's aerial tendencies can be put to good use. Because of this, any young eagle in training should be given the opportunity to soar and develop its skill in the air.

For fitness training, an area of level ground was demanded, but for soaring, just the opposite is required. Uneven country is now desired and, equally important, wind. The effects produced by wind moving over irregular landscapes are varied. In hill country, an experienced eagle will search for lift, recognizing where it is to be obtained, but the young eagle will require guidance. This guidance

51

should be provided by exposing the youngster to only very simple soaring situations. A basic soaring set-up would be a steepish hillside or ridge with a fairly strong wind coming up it from its base (this provides lift). To the falconer more used to flat, open countryside and the confidence this gives, a windy hillside may sound very unappealing. He might imagine the risk of losing his bird is high. But with hand-reared eagles, this is not the dangerous game it might appear to be.

The secret is to introduce the eagle to this kind of thing quite early. As soon as it is responding well to fist and lure and has acquired some basic flying ability, it can slowly be introduced to soaring. Initially, things should be kept as simple as possible. One's aim is to do nothing more than help the bird become familiar with this type of flying. Golden eagles do not need to be taught to soar—this is something they do naturally—but they do require the opportunity to develop this inborn talent.

Just how keen the eagle is to soar will depend a good deal on its nature. Some young eagles are simply more active and aerial than others. Eagles reared in exactly the same way can vary quite considerably in this respect. One bird might only be tempted to soar under ideal conditions; another might find it difficult to sit still at any time! These active birds are the ones I like best. At times, the restless side of their nature can make them a little more difficult to handle, but their desire to fly and keep flying more than makes up for this. At the beginning, they seem to revel in their ability simply to fly; later, they show the same enthusiasm for hunting.

Early soaring sessions will be fairly casual affairs, with the airborne eagle being called in to the fist or lure after a predictable flight of short duration. As the eagle (and falconer) gains confidence, flights will become longer and colored more by the weather conditions and the country being flown over. One training period might see the eagle sailing along a valley side almost level with its owner; another could have the bird holding a position directly above. The height attained during some of these soaring flights needs to be witnessed to be appreciated. So, too, does the hand-reared eagle's response to a lure or training pelt from such a high altitude position.

Eagles with some experience will fold up and drop to earth in a manner that almost defies description. The most spectacular approaches are seen when the bird is directly above its trainer as the lure is exposed. Down it comes in a totally committed stoop. The descent is vertical, with the folded-up eagle growing larger and larger in size as it nears the earth at phenomenal speed. This stoop is held nearly all the way down. There is no lengthy slowing up period: the "brakes" are applied late and the lure taken forcefully.

This type of commitment takes a while to develop and is achieved fastest when the eagle is being flown over familiar ground and especially when the ground contains a single conspicuous building the eagle recognizes as home. Under such conditions, the eagle's attachment to the area acts as a safety net and helps reassure the falconer during these dramatic flights. I have been lucky in this respect and in the past, have trained eagles at two locations where it was possible to allow them to soar almost straight from their perches. In both instances, part of the property looked out over a steep hillside and with the wind blowing up this hill, one had a training arrangement that was difficult to beat.

How much time the falconer devotes to soaring sessions and just what form these sessions take will depend on his ultimate goal. He may have access to vast, open areas of hill country and therefore wish to accustom his bird to hunting solely from aloft. If soaring is viewed simply as a way of rounding off the eagle's education, then its importance may not be quite so significant. But, even in this case, the value of such flying and lure work should not be underestimated. Eagles that have been given a chance to develop their soaring skills and have become used to watching for and coming in at prey from above are simply more rewarding to fly than those that have not. In undulating or even relatively flat country, such a bird will require no urging to take on short scanning flights over hollows or other depressions. In treeless country, these flights begin with the eagle launching out from the fist and returning to it. But in wooded country, a prominent tree might be used as a staging post for similar flights.

Spoiled Eagles

From time to time, one gets inquiries from people who have acquired trained eagles that are proving difficult to work with. In some cases, the falconer's inexperience is the root of the problem and a little advice can ease the situation. However, those that take on eagles from other falconers should be extremely wary about just what kind of bird they are getting involved with. An awful lot of time and effort goes in to producing a manageable hunting eagle and really good eagles are rarely offered openly for sale. Fine birds do change hands, but normally within a circle of friends.

Not so long ago, I was contacted by an English falconer who was experiencing problems with a mature golden eagle he had imported from the Continent. He had obtained this bird at great expense, put it through quarantine and built special housing facilities all on the strength of video footage that showed this bird hunting foxes. But on actually taking delivery of the eagle, he found himself in very deep water. He had flown a variety of other species, but his new acquisition was making his life a misery. He described extremely aggressive behavior, even admitting that the bird had twice chased him off. Flying to the fist was almost impossible and lure work was apparently a nightmare. I offered bits of advice, but made it clear I felt the eagle had been ruined by its previous owner and that the best course of action would be simply to part with it. As tactfully as possible, I asked this troubled fellow why had he not found it odd that this marvelous, supposedly well-mannered, fox-catching eagle had been offered to him. Had the bird been genuine, it would have found a new owner very quickly indeed in its native land. There certainly would have been no need to send it to Britain.

Here, I should make it perfectly clear that the most careful handling in the world will not make a pleasant bird out of a ruined one. Mismanaged eagles that have already developed serious faults are simply not worth having. Of course, slight problems can be nipped in the bud early on in training. But if the bird has been repeatedly robbed on the fist, or had lures or kills forcibly taken from it, then it will almost certainly have acquired some undesirable habits. Attempting to correct these will prove a hopeless challenge. Problem birds can be employed as hunting hawks if extreme caution is exercised, but the experience is hardly a satisfying one. For the falconer whose goals lie beyond simply taking quarry, difficult aggressive birds are of little interest. I would strongly recommend that any falconer contemplating the purchase of a trained or partly trained eagle should first ask to see the bird being handled and flown.

Released Quarries

On the subject of released quarries or bagged game, I intend to say very little. In some countries, this is an acceptable and legitimate part of falconry; in others, it is not. Whether permissible by law or not, the use of released quarries should be conducted with the utmost discretion.

Concluding Note

The training routines detailed in this chapter are designed to develop an eagle that will perform well under a wide variety of conditions. At the same time, the active and stimulating nature of this training will, when coupled with careful handling, produce a bird that is truly enjoyable to work with. There will, of course, be difficult days early on and the falconer should be prepared for the eagle attempting to intimidate him but, if his conviction holds fast, such teething problems will be overcome. Vitally important, however, is that the intensive training program is followed up with an equally concentrated hawking effort. Indeed, in this respect, hunting should be viewed as an extension of training and not a separate issue. It is hunting that really shapes the eagle's character and eventually builds a very special man/bird relationship.

I cannot emphasize how important it is to use the bird for serious hawking. If it is not, then the time and effort devoted to rearing and training will have been wasted. It is here that I would ask the falconer to really search his soul regarding his motives for acquiring an eagle. Are his thoughts really those of a true hunter and if so, are the necessary resources available to provide the bird with regular flights to quarry? The need for an abundance of quarry should not be underestimated as this provides the learning opportunities so vital to a young eagle's development.

5   Practical Hawking Roe Deer and Fox

Roe Deer

Deer hawking with golden eagles is an emotive subject. This is something one has to be aware of when dealing with the topic and pains must be taken to paint a clear and accurate picture of just what the taking of roe deer entail; for this type of hawking is far less shocking and gory than many people seem to imagine.

Those that object to roe deer being taken with eagles often argue that the quarry is simply too large. One well-known falconry figure said she was against roe hawking because the eagle could not kill the quarry cleanly. This is an interesting statement and how many smaller hawks, one might ask, flown to rabbits and hares, kill their quarry cleanly and without assistance? No, in truth, it is more the nature, rather than the size, of the quarry that people react to. People just see deer differently. Also, perhaps some of the old accounts of deer hawking in central Asia have influenced the way people view this aspect of falconry. One observer writing in the 1800s described how an eagle was "tearing out the animal's liver." Even some of the older accounts of deer being attacked by wild eagles can conjure up some frightful visions. For example, one roe deer was said to have been "almost torn in pieces by the eagle."

If an allowance is made for the difference in size, a typical roe flight contains no more violence than the average flight to any large hare species with a goshawk. The bird flies in and subdues (or attempts to subdue) its victim and the falconer hurries to lend assistance. The quarry is not repeatedly hounded or torn into pieces; it is either caught and held, or else it escapes. That said, it would be wrong to imply that deer never sustain any obvious or visible injuries. This can happen, but by and large, roe hawking is not the gruesome affair it is often imagined to be.

What is vitally important is that the falconer knows exactly what to expect and is capable of killing deer quickly. First, the deer will be struggling for its life and will need to be restrained by the falconer himself. This is a physical business; there will be no time for thinking and no time for fumbling about and one needs to act quickly and decisively. If possible, the deer will need to be sat on and a knife quickly used to dispatch it. Just where the knife should be used is a matter of opinion. Some would advise attempting to stab the deer through the heart, but this can be a bloody, drawn out business, especially if one is not sure just exactly where the heart lies. Another method is to force a long, blunt-sided, stiletto-type knife up through the soft under jaw area into the head. An alternative is to put the blade of a knife between the vertebrae below the back of the skull. On paper, this all sounds very straightforward, but in a hawking situation, the inexperienced falconer can easily become flustered and the poor deer will pay the price. If the deer is dispatched correctly, it will not suffer unduly and the scene will not be a gory one.

Perhaps we are getting ahead of ourselves. First of all, we must have an eagle prepared to tackle roe deer, and, unless correctly schooled, many will not. Although not the biggest of deer, the roe is still a large quarry. Its weight runs up to about twenty-five kilograms (in central Europe) and its rather leggy shape can make it look quite intimidating to an inexperienced eagle. When flown at in cover where the roe's bulk is hidden, size is not such an important issue, but out in the open, only the most determined and confident of eagles will take roe on a regular basis.

Regarding the eagle itself, it should not be thought that only the largest female eagles will be capable of taking roe deer. Some of the smaller females can be very effective. Males, too (especially the larger individuals), can account for deer, but the serious deer hawker would be advised to look to female eagles.

When preparing a golden eagle for roe deer, working intensively with suitably large lures is essential. When skinning and jointing a roe for home use, the head should always be left on the pelt and this then popped in the freezer for future use.

Sensible lure work will orientate the bird to deer as a source of food, but the animal's size can still prove a problem. With this in mind, initial hawking attempts should be made in locations where there will be a chance of encountering deer that are only partially visible. This may sound difficult to organize, but with a little planning and luck, it can be achieved. Although sometimes found in open country, the roe deer is an animal linked very much with woodland and it is here that some first class opportunities arise. If the eagle is being flown from the trees, goshawk style, it will have a very good chance of spotting roe deer in or running through cover and such deer will be far more readily taken than those seen in the open.

In areas where fir trees are dominant, flights can be had where man-made clearings in the forest have been replanted and now contain saplings. These young trees provide a carpet of cover for resting roe deer. Invisible until disturbed, these roe deer can be taken with consistency by a trained eagle. Success in these flights depends on several things: how large the clearing is and therefore how far the deer have to travel before reaching the true safety of dense mature forest; the availability of suitable perches for the eagle; and the height of the new plantation itself (sparse, low cover being preferable to closely planted already well-grown trees). The general idea will be to flush deer in a direction that best suits the eagle and this will require a careful approach. Obviously, one wants to avoid allowing deer to escape into the forest out of range of the eagle.

Perhaps an example or two might illustrate this type of hawking more clearly: the eagle has been allowed to take stand in a tree in front of which stretches a fairly narrow plantation of waist- to head-

58

high fir trees. Left and right, the forest is tall and dense. The falconer and two helpers proceed to walk the plantation, moving away from the bird. Almost immediately, a roe deer flushes, breaking left and the eagle, standing tall, spots it and is instantly on the wing. However, the deer is never in any real danger and reaches the cover of the trees before the eagle can close with it. The eagle banks away and lands in a tree on the right-hand side of the clearing. Her position is not a good one, for she is too low and cannot see far enough into the plantation. The falconer recognizes this and considers trying to get the eagle into a better spot; and higher perches are available. Nevertheless, worried that such goings-on will prematurely move any possible quarry, he elects to simply press on. More eager than ever, the hawking party continues to beat through the clearing, but now position themselves more on the left of the plantation. Before long, another deer is moved. This deer, due to the hawking party's position, flushes right. Its path takes it directly below the tree-sitting eagle, which responds immediately. Dropping vertically from its branch, the eagle commits itself fully, but from this angle and at this speed, she is left no room to maneuver. She misses her target by a whisker. Had the eagle been perched higher, she might have seen the quarry sooner and the flight could have had a different ending.

Staying with coniferous forests and young plantations, let us look at another variation on the theme. For this example, we again have a hawking party numbering three and once again, a forest clearing containing young sapling trees. The trees are standing approximately two meters tall and are growing on a gradually sloping hillside. The landscape in general is undulating. The major difference on this occasion is the bird itself. This bird has learned through repeated exposure to similar situations that her best chance of success is not to tree-sit, but to make short, searching, soaring flights over the plantation. Even before the hawking party is amongst the young trees, the eagle is in the air (having left a nearby tree). Her height is not great, perhaps twenty meters and one can clearly see her large head intently scanning the landscape below. Suddenly, she turns over and, folding up completely, drops to earth like a stone. There is a heavy, audible thud and the sound of eagle and quarry crashing about. The unmistakable sound of a roe deer in distress, a half-coughing half-grunting tone, confirms contact has been made. The hawking party is quickly with the bird and find the deer, in this instance a large buck, frantically trying to free itself. The falconer intervenes and ends the competition.

Returning to woodland hawking in general, although woodland flights to roe deer can be extremely interesting, this type of hawking is not entirely without risk. Even a bird the size of a golden eagle can be lost sight of once pursuing quarry; this is especially true when the forest itself is extensive and unbroken and situated in rugged, uneven country. Where flat, wooded country is repeatedly interrupted by river valleys and gorges, roe hawking with golden eagles is inadvisable. Experience has taught me that, in this sort of environment, nothing can be taken for granted, and, even with the simplest of flights, the falconer can quickly lose control of the situation; and, with this type of hawking, control is loose at the best of times.

I have not experienced too many serious problems in woodland, but I have had the odd difficult day and one in particular comes vividly to mind. The weather had been unsettled for several days and very blustery. Conditions were far from perfect for off-the-fist flights in open country and so, desperate to get out, a companion and I decided to try our luck in the nearby forest. By the time we had reached our destination, the wind had picked up, but within the forest we were quite sheltered.

The area itself was not at all dangerous from a hawking point of view as long as one kept away from the single deep valley that cut through the forest. It was to the left of this valley that we eventually found ourselves, and, although our search for quarry had taken us nearer to the "drop off" than I would have liked, I did not feel too uneasy about our position. I had been carrying the bird, a male called Astur, for a while, but now decided to unhood him and release him into the trees, the idea being to try to get him into a suitable position, overlooking what I knew to be a prime spot lying slightly ahead and to our left. Yet, he had no sooner reached a fairly high branch before he was once again on the wing in purposeful hunting flight. From my location, I could see nothing, but my companion gave out the call,

"Roe deer." Hurrying to her position, I could just make Astur out, closing on a single roe, both now nearing the edge of the valley; and at the very point where the flat forest floor fell steeply away, eagle and deer came together. By now, we were frantically running for the spot, but on arriving, out of breath and somewhat anxious, we could see nothing. Then we spied the eagle high above the valley floor and just going into a vertical stoop. Below him was a clearing where an area of trees had been felled and it was in this clearing that the eagle had obviously once again locked on to quarry.

Just what had happened up to this point is difficult to say. My companion had originally seen five or six deer, and, perhaps after losing his chosen victim on the steep slope, the eagle threw up and spotted one of the other fleeing animals. Whatever, the stoop the bird was now committed to was aimed at a target invisible to us, and, as the bird neared the earth, we once again lost sight of him. Slipping and sliding down the valley-side, we made our way as quickly as possible to the opening that lay ahead of us, only to find, once there, that the eagle was again soaring high above the forest, getting plenty of lift from the wind that was now blowing more fiercely than ever.

My companion had already removed the roe deer pelt lure from its carrying bag and was desperately trying to attract the eagle's attention. For a second, it seemed we might be in luck, but no, once again the eagle disappeared from sight. This was serious. Our only chance of retrieving the bird with the lure would have been to use this in open areas, but, in this forest, open spaces were few and far between. With the bird sailing high above the forest canopy and us trapped and hidden below it, things could not have been much worse.

As grim as our position was, two things were in our favor. First, we were not far from home, and, secondly, the bird, who at the time of the incident was eight years old, knew the country intimately and was strongly bonded to the area. I felt it unlikely that he would simply drift off.

Dragging the roe lure behind us, we made our way to the edge of the forest in the general direction of the bird's last known position. Failing to locate him, we moved on and shortly found ourselves in one of our own horse fields. Now, at least we had open ground to work on. The lure, of course, remained visible as we called and scanned the sky, becoming more and more worried. Then, after what seemed an eternity, our luck changed. Some distance away, we could see the eagle soaring above the forest, now higher than ever. He appeared little more than a speck against the clouds. I frantically began to pull the lure across the paddock while my companion kept her eyes on the eagle. He started to respond, coming towards us, but still extremely high. I must have done something like two circuits before, to our relief, he began to make his approach. He came in, not vertically, but very steep and fast. It had been a close call.

There is a point that needs to be made about woodland flying. Any kind of hawking with golden eagles that involves them being given freedom among trees or even perhaps being allowed to soar is not selective. The falconer has absolutely no control over the bird once it spots and begins to fly quarry. In practice, this means that the falconer looking for a female roe deer, say in mid or late November, might find himself bagging a male that has been out of season for a month. Technically speaking, then, any kind of roe hawking that involves having the eagle free should be restricted to times and places where there is no chance of meeting unauthorized quarry (of any kind).

In open country, roe deer are often encountered by chance when the falconer is out looking for hares. It is, in fact, difficult to plan a roe hunt in open country. This is especially true in areas where the deer are primarily woodland dwellers. These woodland deer use open areas to feed at night, but then return to the woods. However, some remain and lie up in cover away from any form of true sanctuary and it is these deer that the hare hawker encounters.

In some areas, roe deer seem to live entirely in the open, having abandoned their woodland roots. For example, in some of the flat, treeless country of eastern Europe, roe deer are abundant. One frequently sees them, mirage-like in the far distance, unconcerned and totally immune to an attack from any trained eagle. Less immune and more vulnerable are those caught "napping" in low ground cover. Up they jump with a start and take off at their best speed; and speed is something the roe deer certainly has, but it may not be enough to save her if she has left her departure too late. She may swing left, she may swing right, but if the falconer is within eighty meters, she will be in serious trouble. Quite long slips are possible at roe deer, depending on the nature of the terrain, but for practical hawking in flat, open country, slipping distances should be kept to under 100 meters.

There have been a number of very successful deer eagles flown in Europe and one of these deserves special mention here, not only because of her effectiveness, but also because of her rather unusual background. The bird, named Lara, was a very small, captive-bred female trained and flown at a castle-*cum*-falconry center in Lower Austria, the Renaissance Falkenhof. Although occasionally used for display work, the bird was also flown for falconry purposes and had been orientated from a very early age to large mammalian quarries (using roe deer pelts).

The story really unfolds at the beginning of the bird's second year. With one hunting season behind her, she was periodically being flown in front of the public, and, one day, during a display and soaring at high altitude, she was lost. Her weight had been taken up to a point where trouble seemed almost inevitable, but no one really expected her to disappear quite so suddenly. She vanished without trace. There was a reported sighting in Germany, another elsewhere, but she was eventually trapped four months later in Poland.

The account of her capture is an interesting tale in itself. It seems that someone wandering in the woods had spotted her and hurried off to tell a local falconer. This falconer dismissed the story of the huge bird, thinking it must be some hawk or buzzard. However, when it was later reported to him that this "buzzard" had now caught a roe deer, he immediately went to investigate. On arriving at the spot, he easily identified the mystery bird as a golden eagle and sure enough, there she was on one very dead roe deer. As he approached, she flew off into a nearby tree, and, although she had what appeared to be an almost full crop, she seemed reluctant to leave the area of the kill. Indeed, it was her keenness to return to the kill that eventually resulted in her being trapped.

So this golden eagle had been free and fending for herself for no less than four months. In open country, she would have surely been shot or suffered some similar fate, but it seems likely that she had been most active in woodland. Here, one can easily imagine that she first preyed on young roe deer (which would have been available to her at the time of her escape) and slowly eased herself into the adult animals as time went by.

Surprisingly enough, once back home, she was not found to be particularly nervous or fearful and it was not too long before she was once again being hunted with. It was at this point that her almost obsessive attraction to roe deer became obvious. In flights from the fist to hares, she was at best mediocre, but when given some freedom in wooded or partially wooded country, her performance against roe deer was devastating. Yet as brutally effective as this small female eagle was, she remained a real pleasure to fly. She was responsive, well-mannered and easy to handle.

In an effort to paint a more vivid picture of this very special eagle and the equally special conditions under which she was trained, I would like to tell of the castle that was and still is, her home. This is a vast place with three inner courtyards. One of these is used for flying displays and another for housing eagles. Both look out over a wooded valley. The third and largest enclosure is the one visitors come into when first entering the castle. This leads directly to the main building, through which guided tours are given. The big courtyard is, except for two gravel paths, fully covered with carefully manicured lawns. During the summer, these lawns are in constant need of repair for they are frequently churned up by horses! It is not unusual for horses to be included in special falconry displays that are arranged throughout the summer, displays that normally have some historical angle. In fact, during the summer, all display work is done with tradition very much in mind. As far as staff is concerned, baseball caps and jeans are out!

What a contrast the winters are. The castle is closed to the public and a skeleton staff keep things ticking over, looking after birds and cutting firewood. Now, bitter winds blow through the still courtyards that were the setting for so much summertime activity and the whole place has a lonely, desolate atmosphere about it. Not menacing or forbidding—simply forgotten. Yes, forgotten is how one feels here in the winter isolated and cocooned in a secret, private world.

But winter comes gradually. First, the castle slowly assumes its autumn mantle and thoughts turn from display work to hunting. Fortunately, the surrounding countryside provides ample opportunities to indulge in serious eagle falconry. Indeed, it is the hawking that sets this place above other establishments I can think of and the hawking that makes this place, to my mind, a true falconry center. This hawking is a very private thing, conducted discreetly by members of staff.

The early autumn and winter of 1993 were no exception. At the castle, the flying display side of things was winding down, but although the frenzied scenes of high summer were over, some fine displays were still being given. The star of the year had been a female imperial eagle and she continued to thrill the now smaller crowds with her incredible flying feats. On a good day, this bird would practically disappear over head in a clear blue sky and come hurtling to earth with such speed and exuberance that one could hear the spectators gasp with astonishment. But as impressive as she was, she shared the spotlight with much larger birds. Griffon and European black vultures were also being flown and these left a very vivid impression on visitors. Flying vultures, especially to and from the fist, is extremely skilled work, but if achieved, the results can be very rewarding. The sight of a huge European black vulture coming into the glove from a high, soaring position is incredible. Growing larger as it descends, the bird resembles a small aircraft.

With the weather cooling and flying displays becoming less frequent, staff were busying themselves with their individual hawking arrangements. There were three golden eagles (including Lara) being prepared for hunting, one of these a first year female. Two falcons were also being worked with. Those interested in hares were fortunate in that more open hunting ground had been obtained where hare numbers were high. The vast forested estate around the castle is not what one would term good hare country; in fact, hares are conspicuous by their absence. On the other hand, the whole area is alive with roe deer and this means regular flights to this fine quarry.

The terrain, too, is sympathetic to the falconer's needs. Although hilly in places, the landscape could in no way be called spectacular, and, apart from the odd rugged corner, it is in fact quite gentle, accessible and walkable by anyone with a reasonable degree of fitness. But what this area lacks in grandeur, it more than makes up for with its tranquillity and sheer beauty. This place is untouched by tourism and visitors to the castle rarely stray beyond the building's boundaries. In winter, the only person one is likely to meet in the forest is an estate worker.

The timber itself is mixed. In places, evergreens predominate, while in other areas, the woodland contains many broad-leaved trees. Yet the landscape, although heavily wooded, is not covered solidly with trees. There are open, grassy pockets, some of them extensive and these add to the pleasure of hawking in this undisturbed place. Roe deer might be the quarry, but the area is home to other animals, the most impressive of these being wild boar. Seldom seen by day, their rummaging nighttime activities and the disturbed forest floor they leave behind remind us of their presence. The forest floor can reveal so much. Roe deer tracks in muddy hollows lure one on and the more adventurous falconer might eventually find himself at the river, overlooking which are the ruins of a long forgotten castle.

The early season of 1993 had been cold and we had experienced many damp and misty days. My girlfriend and I had been living in the outer section of the castle. This part of the building could be cold, but a little discomfort was a small price to pay for the unique feeling these rooms had and the solitude one gained here.

Each morning, our routine was the same. Grab some clothes, get dressed and head across the courtyard to the kitchen and day room, located centrally in the complex. Some mornings, Ivan Maroši would beat us to it and already have the coffee and the wood-burning stove on the go and what a welcome the smell of hot coffee would be.

The day room and kitchen are actually part of a separate mini-complex, which also includes a laundry, a small formal dining room and even a rather stately bedroom. The latter two are rarely used and winter or summer the day room and kitchen form the heart of the establishment. During the summer, these rooms are where rushed members of staff grab a quick break and a bite to eat during a hectic schedule. It is also here in the depths of winter that employees make brief stops to thaw their frozen limbs. One is drawn to the kitchen by coffee and food, but little else. The room itself is pretty nondescript: it could be any kitchen in any household. The day room, on the other hand, makes a very definite statement. This has "falconer" stamped all over it. The room itself is not large and its small size adds to its overall charm. Along one wall is an old sofa, thrown over which is a scruffy sheepskin. There is an ancient wooden cupboard, adorned with hoods and jesses. But what gives the room its real falconry flavor are the old hunting prints, hawking photos and the bits of equipment that hang from them. There is not a patch of bare wall to be seen. Old maps and charts are pinned up all over the place. Some depict the castle and its hunting areas; others show Austria in general. One even pinpoints where hunting and falconry establishments could once be found. The room is used and friendly.

The day room reflects the interests of the center's owner, Josef Hiebeler. One sees his love of tradition and his obsession with the history of falconry everywhere. My association with Hiebeler goes back quite a few years. Our paths first crossed in Germany and we eventually worked together at a falconry center he was running in Bavaria (something about this place appears in a later chapter). Like me, he is very much a practical falconer and we have hunted alongside one another on countless occasions. However, during the autumn and winter of 1993, he found little time for hawking. Most of his days were spent at his home on the outskirts of a nearby village, working on another falconry center project. When not there, he was helping with the construction of breeding enclosures. These were being built away from the main castle in a quiet, walled area and, using existing features wherever possible, they were looking quite attractive. The materials used were, of course, far more robust than they needed to be. As usual, Hiebeler was building something that would last the span of several human lifetimes!

Although other people were on hand during daylight hours, actually living at the castle during this period were just Maroši, my girlfriend and I. This being the case, the day room frequently became something of a "night room." The three of us gathered for some very pleasant evenings and what a fascinating fellow Maroši is. Described as Russian in one book, there seems to be some confusion as to just where he comes from. Pin him down and he will tell you he is Hungarian. He has flown a vast array of birds, but his main experience lies with goshawks and saker falcons. With an intriguing past, he is a treasure trove of interesting tales and stories. One evening, we were treated to an account of his trip to central Asia, but my goodness, it was a lengthy and detailed description. Three bottles of wine later and with us well into the early hours of the morning, he had still not left Vienna airport!

It was a time of both interesting and annoying incidents. For example, Maroši had been away for a few days, and, while he was absent, someone managed to lose his female saker! This put everybody in a bit of a flap. The woods were scoured, look-outs posted, but she was gone. Here, I should add that the saker, although in flying order, was not equipped with telemetry. But fortune was to favor us. A local falconer saw her sitting on a roof top in the next village and she was recovered before Marosi arrived home.

On the plus side, Lara had been in fine form and we enjoyed some very nice roe hunts. The actual flights varied, depending on just where one was. There were long pursuits through open woodland and others that were short and abrupt. One flight was to a roe taken in a deep, overgrown hollow. Disturbed, it had tried to breast the opposite side of the depression, but with Lara already in the air, its fate was sealed. But what a struggle to get to eagle and quarry. The tentacle-like strands of thorns that had hampered the deer also hindered the human in his efforts to reach his prize.

But it is with a more detailed account of a roe hunt that I will bring this section to a close. The day in question was bright and calm, and, by lunchtime, conditions for the hunt were just about perfect.

The eagle looked keen, and, at 3700 grams, she was certainly at the right weight for the task that lay ahead. I had been waiting for castle worker, Andreas Zechmeister. He and I had enjoyed several hunting outings together, but, on this occasion, car trouble prevented him joining me. With this being the case, I roped in another colleague for the trip. Taking Lara on the glove, I gently hooded her and we left for a location where I felt there was a good chance of finding deer.

Outside the castle gates, we turned left and took the narrow, snaking path that wound its way down through the woods. Before long, we turned left again, abandoned the track and made our way across the top of a steepish bank. Our position put us under the castle walls, and, with these towering above, I surveyed the scene ahead. Directly in front of us was a small, square plantation of fir trees. Although quite well-grown, these saplings certainly offered a chance due to the close proximity of the very much taller surrounding trees. The bank we were on assisted the eagle in gaining height, and, with her suitably positioned, my colleague and I were eager to get into the plantation as quickly as possible. This in itself was a little awkward. The bank was smooth and slippery, but with the bird perfectly positioned, it was no time to dally. Sliding down the bank, into the plantation we went. Immediately, we began to beat through the coarse greenery and our rustling prompted the bird to move. She sailed quietly over us and went into another tree. I was now as keyed up as the eagle. Anticipating a flight, I felt charged and positive. In my mind, two things seemed possible. A deer would be either attempted in the plantation and this would require a very steep, totally committed diving attack, or one might be flown at as it evacuated through one of the more open areas of the surrounding mixed woodland. But what a disappointment: as we beat through the plantation it soon became clear that the spot was devoid of roe. There was nothing for it but to call Lara back to the fist and move on.

Our route took us through the woodland in the general direction of the track. In places, the timber was tightly packed and I eased the hooded eagle through, careful not to upset her balance. Any kind of hunting here would have been impossible, which was a pity for we had several sightings of deer.

We moved on and were shortly at a spot where conditions once again made a flight viable. We were overlooking a large, open depression, this containing a private forestry road. Directly below us was an area of tangled cover and opposite this, some distance away, a large plot of young fir trees.

As I released the bird into the trees, my thoughts were more on the rough cover below than on the plantation. A roe breaking from this would provide an ideal opportunity, and, as I crashed my way through the undergrowth, I had high hopes of flushing a deer. What form the action might take was of no great concern. A flight out into the open and across the road would have made a fine spectacle. But from a practical point of view, Lara's location meant that a deer fleeing in almost any direction would have been in fear of its life. Yet here we were once again to be disappointed. However, undeterred and with our minds already on the next possible flight, we began to cross the rough forest road, heading for the young plantation. Rather than retrieve the eagle, I left her to follow on. She was soon with us and she went into a single high tree bordering the saplings. I was almost tempted to leave her where she was, but, on surveying the terrain ahead, I deemed this inadvisable. Our position put us at the bottom of what was in effect a small hill and I knew that, if we were going to fully exploit the situation, we would need to work the plantation from top to bottom, not vice versa. She needed little encouragement to come to the glove, and, hooding her, my companion and I made our way uphill along the perimeter of the tree nursery. We were moving as quietly as possible, but even so, I knew there was a chance that we had already disturbed our intended quarry. Only time would tell.

Long before we reached the top of the hill, I had a rough plan of action in mind. I knew of a shooter's highseat and its location made it an ideal perch for the eagle; from it, the eagle, like the gun hunter, would have a marvelous view of the area below us. Once at the highseat, I had a chance to weigh up the situation more closely. The plantation was far from even: to begin with fairly low, then a middle section of trees that were so high as to obscure the terrain behind

70

them. I felt that, if success was to be had, it would need to be either in front or behind this central bank of higher timber.

With the eagle on the highseat, my companion and I began to walk through the plantation. The atmosphere was tense and the bird was obviously feeling the tension too, for we had not gone far before she left her perch and swept over us in eager anticipation. Her impatience had her repeat this performance twice, both times returning to the highseat. Finally, with the gap between us too great, she went up into a tree a little way back into the forest proper. Then, as my companion and I were approaching the central section of taller trees, the eagle spotted something. Her flight path took her on a long, slanting dive down into the plantation way ahead of us. Due to the tree cover, we did not see her make contact with quarry, but we certainly heard her. Using an arm to protect my eyes, I crashed and stumbled through the barrier of trees that separated us. I was desperate to get to her as quickly as possible, knowing that at any time the quarry could break free. When I reached her, she was hanging onto a large female roe deer with a determination that had become her trademark. Even though she had secured a good head hold, the deer was putting up a terrific struggle and was giving the bird a hard time of it. In the enclosed space the two combatants were in, the scene was one of turmoil, a thrashing tangle of legs, wings and undergrowth. I quickly straddled the deer, going down on my knees and immediately things became a little less chaotic. With the deer pinned by my body weight, I was able to administer the *coup de grace*.

The Red Fox

For many eagle owners, fox flights are something special. Perhaps it has something to do with the fox (like the roe deer) being a traditional golden eagle quarry. Perhaps, too, there is a certain allure for some about flying eagles to animals (be they fox, wolf, or coyote) that are capable of retaliating. With fox hawking, the flight itself is often incidental, the appeal lying more in the bird's ability to overpower a quarry that, although not truly hazardous, is certainly capable of fighting back; and the fox's ability to defend itself should not be underestimated.

The red fox is no weakling, and, if taken incorrectly, is easily capable of freeing itself. At such times, its tactics are forceful and aggressive and the fury displayed becomes more impressive when one considers that this is not a particularly large animal. An average-size male fox from Britain will weigh about 6.5 kg and an average female something like 5.5 kg. (In North America, one finds a wide regional variation in weight, with an overall range of 2.9 kg to 9 kg given.) Nevertheless, for all its spirit, the fox is still quite within the capabilities of an average-size male eagle.

Just how an eagle goes about the business of subduing a fox is a topic that arouses much interest. Some have stated categorically that the quarry is always hit initially in the body and by just one foot, the head being seized a split-second later by the free foot. Others have laid down that, when dealing with aggressive quarries, the eagle plants both feet on the animal's body, then transfers one to the head as the animal attempts to bite. This goes very much against the immediate double-footed head grip detailed in other accounts. In truth, a variety of approaches will be seen and one cannot say without fear of contradiction that one particular type of attack is the rule. It must be remembered that field conditions (the amount of cover or lack of it) will influence how the fox is, or indeed must be, tackled. What can be stated with certainty is that, if the fox is to held, its head and more importantly its jaws, must be brought quickly under control. If the head is not secured, then the fox will bite and snap its way free.

Once taken hold of, the fox's reactions will vary, depending largely on what kind of grip the eagle has secured. One might think that a double head grip will totally immobilize a fox, but this is not the case. A fox taken in this way can be surprisingly active, wrenching and twisting violently. Generally, more control is obtained when the quarry is held by the head and upper body; one foot effectively muzzling the victim, the other driving talons into soft tissue.

Regarding bites, these can and do occur, but fox hawking does not contain the large element of danger that some writers have suggested.

The fox is an extremely adaptable animal and can be encountered in hugely diverse settings. The flights themselves will vary aesthetically, depending on where one is. One might find an early season fox lying out in a low crop on farmland. Off he goes through the cover, and, although only partially visible, his color clashes strongly with the lush, green vegetation. It is a sight that has the eagle pursuing with unbounded enthusiasm. The cover that hid the sleeping fox does not offer enough protection now that the animal is on the move. There are trees ahead, but the eagle drives in to ensure that the fox will never reach them.

Let us now look at another fox flight. For this example, one needs to visualize fairly high, flat agricultural ground, containing a long, wide strip of high, dense cover. At its furthest end, this cover finishes at a point where the land slopes fairly sharply away downhill. At the bottom of this slope (which is more or less devoid of cover), the land evens out, once again becoming flat, open country. Beating through the cover in the direction of the slope walks a small "army" of beaters, these keeping very close to one another. On each side of the strip, an eagle falconer is positioned, these moving in time with the beaters. The idea is to force the fox out into the open, and, as reluctant as he is to leave his hiding place, he is eventually forced to do so. As the party nears the end of the cover, a shout goes up, alerting everyone that the fox is away and is heading downhill at speed. An eagle is shortly on the wing. This is a large male with several foxes to his credit. He is quickly over the hillside and here, high and fully visible to all of the party, he pauses for just a moment. For a second, it seems he has lost sight of his target, which is now almost directly below him and running over flat terrain. But in the time it takes to question his behavior, he closes up and engages the quarry. His attack takes him almost straight down, head first at the fleeing animal. With no cover to protect or hide it, the fox is overcome by the eagle's sledge-hammer tactics. But this is no reckless assault: the head hold is clamped on, and, although the fox is far from finished, it is held until a hunting knife concludes the matter.

The fox is not renowned for its speed, but it is a master at weaving through the sparsest of cover while keeping itself largely concealed. I recall an incident that illustrates just how elusive the fox can be. Some colleagues and I were in Hungary looking for hares and the fox provided an interesting diversion. With an abundance of quarry and ideal landscapes to fly over, the trip was living up to our expectations. Hawking in Hungary really is a treat. Home to the Great Plain and also central Europe's largest lake, this intriguing land has much to offer the contemporary falconer. How can one hawk here without thinking of falconers such as George Lelovich and Lorant de Bastyai, who enjoyed so much fine hawking at a time when the world in general had a slower pace? Their descriptions of hunting from horseback and flights across the Great Plain brought the delights of Hungary to the attention of others. Even today, this land is extremely compatible with falconry, and, in some areas, flights from horseback are still quite feasible.

Winters in Hungary are severe, but on this particular trip we were enjoying mild early season weather. The fox flight occurred during an afternoon that found a group of us hawking over extensive, flat country. We were proceeding through a massive area of patchy, thigh-high cover. The group was somewhat strung out and my position had me off to the right. Way off to the left, I saw two companions both attempt flights at a quarry not visible to me. As we proceeded, I witnessed several of these unsuccessful flights, each time the birds returning to their owners. I presumed my fellow falconers were flying at hares, although the activity I was observing had me somewhat puzzled. Shortly, I caught glimpse of a fox (this too being off to my left) and I quickly released my eagle. The fox was some distance away, but the bird, skimming over the cover, was locked on and committed. He took the fox, but failed to hold it and Raynard disappeared once again among the cover. My companions and I now came together to discuss the incident and it was then I learned that the flights I had earlier witnessed had in fact been to this very same fox. He had been ahead of our party for goodness knows how long, never really exposing himself to danger until this final unsuccessful flight.

The fox has remained a valued eagle quarry in central Asia, and, in parts of Kazakhstan, mounted falconers go about fox hawking in a rather unique way. Riding ridges and hillsides, they occasionally pause and unhood their eagles. The idea is to allow the eagle itself to scan for quarry rather than the falconer relying solely on his own eyesight. From a high vantage point, the eagle is able to spot the slightest movement, and, in river valleys where undergrowth provides the quarry with ample refuge, the eagle's assistance really is essential. This method proves far more successful than simply riding across the open steppe hoping for an encounter.

A few years ago, a colleague of mine, Andreas Zechmeister, whom I mentioned in the roe deer section, was lucky enough to see Kazakh falconers in action first hand. He traveled to Kazakhstan with four German friends (he himself is Austrian), and, with the help of Dr. R. Pfeffer, who acted as translator and guide, he was afforded a glimpse of central Asian eagle falconry. Dr. Pfeffer played a vital role. At the time, he was working for Alma Ata zoo as an ornithologist and was spending a great deal of time in the field studying wild raptors. He had an intimate knowledge of certain parts of Kazakhstan and also had direct contact with several falconers.

Zechmeister made some interesting observations during his four-week trip and the following is a translation of an account he gave me:

"The setting for our fox hawking expedition was south-eastern Kazakhstan. To the south lay Kirghizstan, to the east China. The area in question is overshadowed by the massive Tian Shan mountains which rise to towering peaks. Our base camp comprised of three *yurts*. Sometimes called *auls*, these are the traditional home of central Asian nomads. Round, tent-like structures, *yurts* have been used as dwellings for centuries by the wandering peoples of the steppe. It was from this camp that we were led on daily hunting excursions. These mounted trips were long, averaging perhaps thirty-five kilometers a day and took us over the hilly ground leading up to the Tian Shan.

"The month was November, bitterly cold by night but by day quite warm. The nighttime cold was emphasized on our first evening when the whole group, exhausted as we were, had to deal with a snow storm which blew part of the *yurt* away. With low evening temperatures some form of heating was, of course, essential and this was provided by a small oven, fueled by dried animal dung.

"Several sights left me with vivid impressions. Very memorable was our first morning. I recall emerging from the *yurt* to bright sunshine and the sight of our horses tied to the tethering pole. This pole deserves special mention. The lack of wood on the open steppe means that this well used length of timber needs to be transported with the group each time the camp is altered. At a new site it is simply buried in the ground.

"For our initial hunt we were accompanied by three Kazakh falconers with three eagles. Our route took us over rough ground, cut through by numerous small valleys. Where rocky outcrops offered sufficient protection from the elements, bushy vegetation occurred. Some of my colleagues were finding the going difficult and as we approached the scene of the first flight I found myself alone with our Kazakh guide and head falconer, Machan. The flight in question had, for me, a rather unusual beginning. Machan began to shout peculiar hunting calls and aimed these at an area of dense scrub beneath us. What happened next was surprising to say the least. His blood curdling cries caused a fox to leave its hiding place (this calling as I later learned was quite common practice). The fox ran up the hill-side, over the top and down into the next valley. My guide called out 'fox,' unhooded his eagle and let her fly. The flight began slightly downhill, going across the hillside. To begin with the eagle was simply gaining ground from behind. But as the fox made level terrain the eagle attained a bit of height, turned over and came straight down at it from above.

"From where I was I could see the quarry had been taken and so I urged my horse on. In places the ground was frozen and this made riding at any kind of speed difficult. I was eager to get to the scene of the kill as quickly as possible but had no desire to put myself or my horse at risk. Machan took a slightly different route and arrived on the spot before me. However, I was not far behind and joined him as he dispatched the fox. His big female eagle had obtained a perfect double-footed head grip and was soon being rewarded for her efforts.

"For me it had been important to be present at the scene of the kill and not be some distant spectator. By keeping up with my Kazakh host I hoped that somehow he would accept me more as a fellow hunter and horseman. The fox was bound to the horse behind the saddle and as the rest of the party joined us, we prepared to move on.

"Our horses were quite varied in terms of breeding. Some were typical Kazakh hunting ponies, small, tough and capable of carrying a rider over the most treacherous terrain. Others were larger containing Don blood. The Don is a horse long associated with Cossack riders and a breed famed for its powers of endurance. What struck me was that very little attention was paid to the horses. They were left saddled for many hours and simply hobbled for convenience.

"The eagles being flown were all wild trapped birds and kept in quite a low condition. Because of their low condition it was important to obtain downhill or across hill flights. On the subject of flights, I was amazed to see that all the birds were actually being flown with leashes attached to their jesses. The leash was used as a means of securing the bird after an unsuccessful flight. The falconer would ease up to his bird and get hold of the leash. The eagles were not called back to their owners but more often than not had to be retrieved. These Kazakh eagles were carried on the right hand and each falconer used a three fingered, mitten-type glove; this fur lined against the cold.

"Like the horses, the eagles were given little consideration when not being hunted with. They spent most of their time hooded and were dotted about the camp wherever a convenient perch could be found. No true blocks or perches were used. Saddles, stools, even mounds of earth were employed instead. More care was taken with the eagles when out hunting. Already in a weakened condition it was vitally important that they should not waste their energy reserves simply trying to remain on the rider's fist. A slow, steady pace was required. It is worth mentioning that female eagles were prized far more highly than males. The only male eagle present was being handled by Machan's son. But whether male or female I noticed that these birds were much larger than the ones I was more familiar with.

"We spent six days at our first camp, traveling out each day on horseback to hunt. Then we moved on, air-lifted by helicopter and flown some 300 kilometers to another base. This camp was most interesting. It was set up around a spring over which stood a single huge tree. This tree contained an old imperial eagle's nest. Again *yurts* were our accommodation, two for living in, one for cooking.

"It was at this second camp I had the opportunity to take part in a sight hound hunt. For this the eagles were left at camp and I was given a shot-gun to carry. With the shot-gun came the order 'if you see a wild dog shoot it.' Apparently in this area feral dogs had become a problem for shepherds and a direct course of action was being taken. We were a party of four riders and two lean sight hounds. The weather for this hunt was very inhospitable with strong winds and freezing conditions. The ground itself was flat and marshy containing high, coarse grass. In places this marshland was frozen, unattractive to the eye and after four hours in the saddle under bitter conditions it became a loathsome place. To make things worse only one feral dog and a single fox were seen, but neither was caught or shot. The day remains vivid due to one incident. At one point a small icy river had to be crossed. This was only perhaps 4 meters wide but quite deep, so deep in fact that legs had to be hoisted out of stirrups to prevent them becoming soaked. On the opposite bank the wind chill resulted in our horses' tails being almost frozen solid. The dogs were most unhappy. Both made it across the river but on the other side were huddled and obviously in distress. Just how much the river crossing had taken out of them soon became clear. One managed to keep up with the party, but the other was left behind and was eventually lost. The loss of this dog did not at all concern our Kazakh host.

"From camp number two our daily excursions took us into areas where foxes were more abundant. One hunt found us in a landscape of wide, shallow valleys, through which wound small streams. Left and right of these streams the immediate ground was uneven but as one followed the valley side up, moving away from the water, the gradual climb saw one eventually in flat, steppe country. We were riding along a ridge overlooking a stream when two foxes flushed from cover. They were some way ahead and below us. For a little way the foxes remained together but then took separate routes. One was lost but the other remained in view and was making its way uphill. An eagle was slipped and again the quarry was taken from above. This fox was actually given to me and back at base it was skinned enabling me to bring the pelt home. Today it remains a prized possession and continually reminds me of this extremely special trip."

6   Hare Hawking

The brown hare has a widespread distribution across the Old World. Outside of its natural range, it has been artificially introduced to a number of places, for example, North America and New Zealand. In Europe, it is an animal associated strongly with agricultural land-scapes, although really this hare is well adapted to open steppe-type country. A study in southern England indicated that brown hares fared best where fields were smallish and crops varied. Nevertheless, in parts of continental Europe hares can be found in large numbers where fields are very big, even vast and crop types simplified.

A sizable lagomorph, an adult brown hare from Britain or central Europe will weigh about 3.5 kg, with the odd individual weighing much more. Brown hares of over 5 kg do occur. With such size, this hare is a much larger animal than the European rabbit, which weighs in at about 1.5 kg. It also differs from the rabbit in build. The brown hare is lean and leggy and when moving at slower speeds can appear almost antelope-like. By comparison, the rabbit is a more compact creature.

The brown hare is surely one of nature's greatest achievements. Able to reach speeds of fifty-five to seventy kilometers per hour and gifted with truly amazing agility, is it any wonder that this creature has fascinated hunters and naturalists alike throughout the ages? The literature on the brown hare is extensive and her praises have been sung many times. In *The Master of Game* (written between 1406 and 1413), she is described, quite fittingly, as "...the most marvelous beast that is."

Many of the older accounts of hare hunting concern themselves with the use of sight and scent hounds; and the hare has always been a highly esteemed "longdog" quarry. But the hare was not overlooked by early hunters using trained hawks and hare hawking is a very traditional kind of falconry. In fact, whether encountered in desert or steppe country, or on snow-covered mountain slopes, hares of one type or another have long been a target for the huntsman's hawk.

My own interest in the brown hare goes back to my earliest days in the sport, and, over the years, I have flown most of the European and North American birds associated with this quarry. I have not hunted the brown hare in North America, but have pursued it over much of its European range. My experiences have been as varied as the terrain flown over and the birds used. There have been long-range flights with ferruginous hawks on disused airfields, days spent in search of woodland hares with female goshawks and hunts across sweeping hare-rich arable landscapes with golden eagles.

It has been in the company of golden eagles that I have enjoyed the most memorable sport, and, for intensive hare hawking, the eagle really is in a class of its own. That said, developing a truly effective hare-catching eagle takes time and dedication. For the inexperienced bird, the challenge with this quarry lies not in subduing it, but in actually catching it to begin with; young golden eagles normally find all but the most straightforward flights difficult.

If any real success is to be achieved against brown hares with a young golden eagle, then the key is to get out into the field early in the season. At this time of year, the inexperienced eagle will be faced with equally inexperienced prey and this is a most important factor in obtaining success. A midwinter hare might look very much like its early season counterpart, but it is quite a different animal.

Early in the season, one will also have a better chance of finding hares in sufficient numbers; and the young eagle will need all the practice it can get. Here, a word of warning. An abundance of hares does not mean that the bird should be slipped at each and every hare that gets up no matter what its position: this will lead to discouragement. No, the real beauty in having a lot of hares is that ideal slips can be chosen and the bird provided with the very best chances.

So just what would be considered a suitable slip? First of all, let me say that this question is far less straightforward than it might first appear. I am always most reluctant to lay down specific slipping distances because, without additional information, a measurement of distance means very little. In the field, the performance of both pursued and pursuer will be affected by various influences, such as ground conditions and wind direction and strength. The hare's speed and maneuverability will be governed by the terrain it is running over. On flat, smooth ground, the brown hare comes into her own and can be extremely evasive. On rough, broken ground (for example, a deeply furrowed field), things will be less to her liking. The eagle, on the other hand, will not at all be troubled by the terrain, but certainly will be affected by wind conditions. Flights into the wind are always the falconer's least desirable option.

With time and practice, the falconer will develop a feeling for when a slip is viable or not. He will assess the overall picture and notice things the less experienced falconer may not see. For example, not only the nature of the ground the hare is running on, but also the kind of terrain she is approaching. Then there is her speed: is she panicked and sprinting, or moving slowly at some distance? He will also note his own position in relation to the quarry (he may be on higher ground). Then there will be the bird to consider: its age and experience and how well it knows the quarry. For the bird, too, will learn to understand when things are in its favor. These points and more will be assessed in a split second by the experienced falconer.

As can be seen, the giving of accurate slipping distances is an almost impossible task. Nevertheless, if the reader feels he must have a few measurements for reference, the following guidelines may be of help. Slips of 200 meters or more can result in success, but the novice hare hawker would be advised to keep distances down to around fifty or sixty meters.

Now to look at hare hawking in general. Normally speaking, hares will be more approachable (and therefore shorter slips will be had) when there is some type of ground cover. Early in the season, root crops can provide excellent opportunities and nothing seems to excite an eagle more than a big brown hare rustling away through a patch of roots. Root crops come in all shapes and sizes and the term "roots" might be used to describe crops such as sugar-beet, swedes or turnips. All have an edible root and a leafy protruding top and it is this above ground vegetation that provides the hare with a feeling of security. Shortish slips are also frequently to be had on rough, ploughed fields. What one wants is a field that has been ploughed in deep furrows and left. Less desirable are freshly worked areas where the resident hares will have had their routines disrupted.

Another opportunity one could consider favorable is when a hare is located lying tight in her form. Brown hares do not use burrows as European rabbits do, but, in open country, they will make slight depressions or hollows in which they can lie. These forms provide a method of concealment and also give the hare some protection from the elements. If a hare is spotted in her form, things should not be rushed. First, note which way she is facing and therefore which way she is likely to run. Secondly, I would advise backing off a little, and, if possible, getting someone else to flush the hare. It might seem that the closer one can get to her the better, but this is not the case. Hares can be easily missed when they are simply put up from underfoot. Often, the eagle overflies them as they put in a first quick turn. It is worth mentioning that hares can sometimes be steered in a direction more favorable to the falconer. If the hare is facing the "wrong" way (e.g. into a strong wind), the falconer can skirt round, allowing plenty of room, and attempt to push her in another direction. This, of course, is more feasible if one has help. With squatting hares, if the eagle is being flown out of the hood (this will be looked at shortly), the hood will be left on until the falconer is in position and removed just prior to the hare being flushed.

Although it is only a depression in the ground, a form can keep a hare surprisingly well hidden. A casual observer can scan a flat, smooth field containing several hares and see nothing. That said, it is sometimes possible to spy the small amount of earth pushed up out of a form from quite a distance. Such irregularities give away the hare's secret to the falconer with a practiced eye. I have personally found forms most visible late in the season when fields have been ploughed and seeded and winter wheat is just poking through the surface.

Of course, it is not only soil disturbance that can betray a hare's presence. Under conditions of fresh snow, the slightest thing out of the ordinary can be most conspicuous. On a white, flat landscape, even a feature as seemingly unimportant as a small mound of snow will draw the hunter's attention. Nevertheless, if the snow is sufficiently deep, the hare herself, although brown in color, will be invisible in her snow form to any distant observer.

Less invisible is a squatting hare to the airborne eagle. It is not unusual for an experienced eagle, having missed one hare, to gain a little height and spot another. When the terrain is undulating and the eagle is being provided with some lift, the scene is set for such incidents.

Successful hare hawking with golden eagles relies very much on planning. There is far more to it than simply wandering about the countryside in hope of encountering hares in suitable positions. The fact that the eagle's performance will be influenced by the wind has been mentioned and this topic now needs a closer examination. In flat, open country, the wind can often be something of a problem. Even a very fit eagle slipped against a strong wind will have little chance of making contact with its quarry. On windy days, there are only two ways to go about things: one either hunts with, or across, the wind. Downwind flights can be very fast, but for this speed, the bird sacrifices control. With the wind behind it, an eagle can eat up huge distances, but its maneuverability will be greatly reduced.

Even when downwind flights are deemed advisable, one cannot hawk downwind all day. Sooner or later, the falconer will need to do an about turn (if he wants to return home, that is!) and will be faced with hawking against the wind. If help is at hand, he may want to attempt cross-wind flights. These flights can be obtained by the falconer positioning himself left or right of the beaters and some way ahead, with the whole party, of course, heading into the wind. Any hares flushed by the beaters can be "cut off" by the forward-positioned falconer slipping across the field.

When flying from the fist over uneven terrain, positioning is also an important issue. If the falconer is out in company, he should be constantly checking that his position in relation to this company and any likely looking hare spots is favorable. Let us imagine that ahead of the hawking party the ground forms a large, shallow depression. The terrain in general looks rather uninviting, having no cover at all. In the hollow, however, is a narrowish strip of dying vegetation and it seems likely that, if any hares are to be found, this is where they will be. The falconer may be tempted to take up a central position and, with beaters each side of him, walk the cover. This would be a bad move, due to the fact that left and right to him the ground runs away uphill. A far better position would be on either side of this cover strip and actually some distance away from his helpers. From such a location, his eagle will have a far greater effective range.

Where isolated clumps of trees relieve open agricultural ground, the hare hawker is presented with a situation not to be wasted. Brown hares frequently shelter within the cover of trees, especially during periods of harsh weather and so pockets of timber must always be approached with caution. The best procedure is to release the eagle into the trees before venturing too near. If the eagle has been accustomed to working from trees, it should need little encouragement to take a suitable perch. A hare may flush before the falconer actually reaches the tree line or a little rummaging around may be required. Whichever proves to be the case, the eagle will be far better positioned in a tree than on its owner's fist. Even when cover situations like this result in no hares being flushed, there may very well be a hare lying out in the field quite near to the trees. A hare trying to obtain a little shelter from the wind and weather in this way might also provide a flight for a tree-sitting eagle.

Writing this, I am reminded of an occasion when things did not run quite to plan. It was at the beginning of an afternoon's hare hawking, which saw a friend and I out with a male eagle. A few hundred meters from where we had parked our vehicle was a fairly narrowish section of mature, broad-leaved woodland, this growing along both sides of a large and steep-sided gully. Actually, this gully appeared oddly out of place, dissecting as it did gently rolling, open arable land. The day was bitterly cold, wind-still and the ground frozen rock hard.

We made our way directly to the trees, and, as we were in good hare country, I half-expected to put up a hare before we reached them. But this proved not to be the case, and, on nearing the tall standing timber, I allowed the bird to fly in and select his own position. We quickened our pace and were shortly at the edge of the gully. As no quarry had moved or been sighted, my companion and I proceeded to beat along the tree line, expecting the eagle to follow. Stimulated by our activity, the eagle changed trees and quickly spotted something way out on the open ground opposite us.

Although the trees had long since shed their leaves, this small strip of woodland was fairly dense and our view of the eagle as it launched out across the field was restricted. Initially, I was more intrigued than anything else: where was the bird's intended victim? What I could see of the field was totally bare and there was no sign of any fleeing quarry. However, I had assumed that the eagle's target was a nearby hare and in this assumption, I was wrong. With the advantage of height, he had obviously spotted something a long way off and it was now clear that his flight path, if held, would take him a considerable distance. The priority was to keep him in sight and this was proving difficult through the trees. I had to get after him and it was now that the gully I had so keenly sought out become a treacherous hindrance. It had to be crossed and quickly.

With a sense of urgency building inside me, into the mini-ravine I went. The sliding in was none to difficult, but the climbing out was more of a chore. With the "obstacle" negotiated, I was relieved to see the bird sitting on the ground—a long way off, yes, but no longer in flight. Whatever he had been after, he had missed. The terrain between the eagle and me ran very slightly uphill (this had not affected the eagle's flight, due to the elevated perch he had initially held) and the eagle now occupied the highest point visible.

Before I could call him to the glove, he flew up onto what appeared to be a pile of stacked logs. Call him as I did, his attention had been drawn by something more interesting and off he went again, disappearing over the rise. This all happened very quickly indeed, and, with my companion still in the gully, I set off running with purpose. Luckily for me, the frozen, bare terrain was fairly smooth. Lungs bursting, I reached the top of the rise to see the eagle struggling with a hare on a newly sprouting winter crop. Having taken the hare badly, he needed help and he needed it quickly. But he was far away and I was exhausted. I simply could not run any more, and, although I gave my best effort, the hare broke free and escaped long before I was on the scene. I am sure that the account of this exhausting hunt would no doubt put most falconers off using trees as hunting aids. However, let me emphasize that the type of incident described was meant to illustrate the exception rather than the rule.

After discussing slipping distances and outlining one or two field procedures, I feel it important to include something on the flights themselves. What can the falconer expect to see once a hare is up and running? Well, this is almost as difficult to outline as the business of slipping distances (and of course, the two topics are linked). One pursuit might see the eagle closing on a long-range hare that seems to be almost "picking" its way across broken ground. Another flight could see eagle and hare going hell for leather down-hill. These frantic downhill pursuits can result in some spectacular action. The hare can sometimes be dragged almost clear from the ground before prey and predator come to rest, or eagle and hare might come together at full speed, only to cartwheel over in a cloud of dust.

The simplest flights will see a hare put up close (or flushed from its form) and taken in a direct, straight-line pursuit. Not at all interesting to watch and hardly demanding on the bird. More demanding is the hare, perhaps flushed at a greater range, that veers off sharply to the left or right as the eagle closes with it. This abrupt change of direction might bring an end to the flight, with the eagle overshooting to become grounded. On the other hand, it might be the beginning of a more lengthy affair, with a persistent eagle staying on the wing and attempting to match several such maneuvers. These testing calculated competitions are very enjoyable to watch.

Another flight could see the hare (after being missed) spin right round and head back in the direction she came from. In this way, a short flight into (or across) the wind can result in a downwind flight; and the eagle that was unsuccessful with its first attack might take the hare on its second attempt. Sometimes, when being closely pursued in open country, a hare will stop dead and flatten out just ahead of the eagle. This can result in a nice flight sequence, with the bird throwing up above its target and coming straight back down at it.

The most effective and spectacular anti-eagle maneuver employed by the brown hare is a vertical jump. Just when it seems that the hare will surely be taken, she launches herself skyward with a suddenness that leaves the eagle completely baffled. The falconer will be surprised, too, for there is no indication that this tactic is about to be employed. There is no build-up. This is not some last-ditch attempt to shake off a persistent pursuer. It is one move on its own and normally the culmination of the simplest of flights.

It is not always the hare's acrobatic ability that saves it from capture; sometimes, ground vegetation will aid the hare in her escape. While it is true that short slips and successful flights can often be had in cover, depending on the density and depth of the vegetation, the eagle can find it difficult to actually get to grips with its intended victim.

When flying hares that are running through ground cover, some eagles fare better than others. Some eagles just seem to develop a technique for taking fast, partially visible hares; at the same time, such a bird may not perform as well as another in perfectly open country. Because of these strengths and weaknesses, the prevailing hunting conditions during any given days sport may favor one bird more than another, but I have never seen this demonstrated quite so dramatically as during one particular afternoon's hare hawking. This was a few seasons ago in Hungary and I was attending an official falconry meeting.

The meeting was an interesting affair. Three days were set aside for hunting and the base for the gathering was what appeared to be a one-time military camp, complete with barracks and mess-hall. It has to be said that the place itself was a little gray and dreary and although all the necessary facilities were on hand, things were pretty basic. If anything, however, this added to the overall appeal, especially with so many colorful characters in attendance.

Sadly, the first couple of days were spoilt for me because of ill health. I had been none too good before leaving Austria, and, once in Hungary, the physical business of hunting had made me feel worse. This had been reflected in my hawking. My reactions were pathetic and the one hare I did manage to bag was taken more by luck than skill on my part. But then, on the morning of the third hunting day, things took a sudden turn for the better. I woke up feeling 100 percent fit. The shakes, shivers and stomach pains had gone and I felt incredibly positive.

As it turned out, the morning proved to be fairly uneventful, but during the afternoon, the small group I found myself in was treated to some fine sport. The party contained two other eagle owners (these being German), a number of Hungarian beaters and four Italian gentlemen who were flying falcons. We looked a rather interesting group, but before I explain how we decided to operate, let me first describe the landscape. We were on very open, flat agricultural ground devoid, for the most part, of any form of cover. Indeed, in the immediate foreground were totally smooth, bare earth fields, these, like the rest of the countryside, being unfenced. It would have made a pretty unappealing picture except for one thing. Slap bang in the middle of this emptiness was a huge square patch of low, dark green vegetation. This oasis looked so good I swear I could actually smell the hiding hares! Our exact location put us not too far from a place called Hodmezovasarhely and quite near the Romanian border.

It was fairly obvious to all concerned that we should restrict our efforts to the tempting green area and ignore the surrounding, less inviting terrain. The plan was straightforward. We would simply line up, keeping close and walk the field back and forth in sections. By doing this we hoped to miss as few hares as possible. Also, to avoid any problems (that is, falcon/eagle confrontations), it was decided to initially leave the falcons in one of the vehicles.

From our parking place, along an agricultural track, the vegetation in the field had looked like fairly "standard," calf-length cover. On getting up to it, I fully expected to find a crop I was familiar with, but I must confess, on closer examination, I was completely baffled. That it was a crop of some sort was fairly certain, but just what it was or what it was going to grow into was a mystery to me (and indeed to my German colleagues). The Hungarian description of it left me more confused than ever! Rather than having a fairly uniform look about it, the crop was quite patchy and uneven in places. Also, its rather coarse texture was different from anything I had come across before. But it was cover, it was low and, like the rest of the party, I was itching to see what it held.

The eagle I was flying at this particular meeting had come from an Austrian friend whose work in the police force had made flying an eagle impossible; his free time was simply too short. I must say that he was not the easiest of birds to work with. He was not aggressive, but not a bird to take liberties with and I suppose, if I had to be honest, not the type of bird one easily gets attached to. But he had plus points. Flying now in his third season, he was becoming something of a hare specialist and had a knack for taking hares in cover.

If I had felt positive earlier in the day, then now I felt doubly so. The weather was fine and bright, there was very little wind and in front of me was what appeared to be a little bit of hare hawker's heaven.

We had all expected to find a good number of hares and we were not disappointed. Walking slowly and carefully, we were flushing them at quite regular intervals. Yet, it soon became apparent that the unfamiliar cover was causing problems for the birds. The two German falconers off to my right were having no end of bad luck. I was doing a little better, and, although my bird had also experienced its fair share of near misses, by the time we had reached the other end of the field, he had taken two hares. One of these was put up inadvertently by the Italian gentleman on my right when he stopped to remove a camera from his rucksack. Had he not stopped, we would have simply walked over the tightly squatting animal, just as we had no doubt walked over others.

I put my two successful flights down to luck. The cover was perhaps a little more patchy in my part of the field and this had made things easier for the eagle. Nevertheless, my eagle's third hare, taken on the way back down the field, had nothing to do with luck. Now all the eagles were hunting under exactly the same conditions. Interesting was the fact that there seemed to be no obvious reason why my eagle was doing better than the others (and I knew one to be a very experienced bird). All of the flights, successful and otherwise, were quite similar in style. They were brisk flights with the hares tending to swing left or right across the field. This made for long, curving pursuits, the eagle keeping fairly low as it followed the quarry's line. Of the hare itself, the human observer caught only fleeting, interrupted sightings and at the end of each flight, for a split second, one was not sure if the bird had hit its mark or not. Those hares that were missed near to where the bare earth fields began would be seen heading out across open ground, moving quickly, but no longer under pressure. Other hares, put up and missed deeper within the square of cover, were simply lost track of.

Our walk through the second section of the field brought us back to the vehicles, and, on reaching these, it was decided to give the falcon enthusiasts a chance to fly their birds. Apparently, one or two pheasants had been spotted entering a rough and neglected corner of the field and this set-up, it was hoped, would provide a successful flight for a hybrid falcon. A pheasant was in fact located by one of the Italians' dogs and a firm point obtained. But, the falcon never came into a suitable position for the flush and simply drifted off, requiring her owner and his assistants to go in search of her.

So now with the Italians occupied with the business of retrieving their troublesome bird, my German colleagues and I (and our Hungarian helpers) resumed our search for hares. Back up the field we went and the story proved very much the same. Some unsuccessful flights by the other eagles and another hare for mine. This was becoming embarrassing. However, the situation was eased when one of the other eagles took a roe deer. This deer was disturbed as it lay in some of the thicker cover. It was a fine, long flight, displaying very nicely how effective an eagle can be against large quarry. It also emphasized how difficult the hares were proving to be for even a very committed bird.

Although the hare flights we were seeing were of a direct nature and fairly low level, my own bird's return to the fist, following any unsuccessful flights, was tending to be a little less direct. By now, there was a slight breeze and he was making full use of it. On at least three of his return flights, he sailed lazily over the hawking party before coming into the glove. This scanning behavior was fairly typical for him and I knew he was hoping to either spot a hare for himself, or have one flushed while he was in the air. Even in this flat, featureless area, he could not resist attempting to employ this tactic. But his efforts were wasted and all of the hares he took, including the fifth and final one, were taken in direct flights from the fist.

During a relatively short afternoon's hawking, this male eagle had accounted for all of the five hares bagged. It had been a very interesting day due to the strange conditions and the way in which the hunt had progressed; and for me, a meeting that had initially begun as a bit of an endurance test had an unexpected and rewarding conclusion.

Flying "Out of the Hood"

When one thinks of out-of-the-hood flights, falcons come more readily to mind than golden eagles. Nevertheless, this technique is also widely employed by those working with eagles and at times, flying out of the hood has definite advantages over the approach that sees the bird carried unhooded in the field. Hare hawking in a group situation is a good example of this. While waiting for its turn, the unhooded eagle must watch other birds pursue quarry that it would dearly love to chase. The hooded eagle sits calmly on its owner's fist, oblivious to the goings-on around it and ready to give its best when finally slipped. Even when one is hawking alone, the use of a hood prevents the eagle becoming restless and attempting to fly quarry that is out of range. Flying out of the hood has just one disadvantage when hawking hares: the unhooded eagle might well spot the odd hare sitting tight in its form, but the hooded eagle cannot.

It has been argued (by those who do not hood their eagles) that the unhooded eagle can react faster than its hooded counterpart. Here, of course, much depends on the individual falconer: how quickly he can assess a potential slip and how well he has prepared the eagle. The skilled falconer makes it look easy and never seems short of either opportunities or time. There is a calm air about him as he selects prime slips from the less desirable ones. Yet there is nothing calm about this falconer's eagle once its hood is removed. It reacts instantly. There is no hesitation: one moment it is sitting statue-like on its trainer's arm, the next powering away after quarry.

If a hood has been used throughout the eagle's early training period, then the foundation for out-of-the-hood flights will be in place. Lure work, especially the fast, motorized kind, prepares the eagle well for true hunting situations. Naturally, the eagle differentiates between lifeless lures and real quarry (as it does between hunting and training sessions in general), but it learns to associate the removal of the hood with serious pursuit flights. Its hood is quickly removed and it expects to see potential prey. One simply builds on this when hunting by flying in good hare country and providing the bird with sensible slips.

Just what kind of hood is used for this type of hawking is a matter of choice. Having no braces, central Asian eagle hoods work well, but the fit must be perfect. If a hood with braces is being used, then these should be adjusted to keep the hood on, but not prevent its instant removal. As with an Asian hood, its fit must be perfect even when "ready for action." If it is constantly moving and irritating the eagle, it is not suitable. Even a well-fitting hood can move when in a partially opened position and so, if the bird suddenly becomes a little restless during a day's hawking, the hood should be looked to first.

Wet Weather

Most eagle owners I am sure would consider hawking under wet conditions unappealing. The main problem is that the bird's performance is severely affected when its plumage becomes wet, and in heavy rain the bird can become wet before it even flies. Even if the rain itself should stop, the ground will be saturated and should the eagle come into contact with this after an unsuccessful flight, this too will wet its plumage. When flying over low crops or other moisture holding vegetation an unsuccessful flight can spell disaster. If one or two similar flights follow then the bedraggled bird may as well be carried home. It is surprising how performance is affected by wet feathers. The eagle that was brisk and sharp in flight becomes a powerless, unmaneuverable pudding! That it is at a disadvantage is all too clear to the bird too, for mentally one sees it switch off. The intensity goes and the pursuits become half-hearted.

Wet conditions also influence hare numbers. Hares will move off open, water-logged ground and head for the hedgerows. This is not to say that these animals will not be found on wet fields or even lying in thick, saturated crops, but they will not be found in large numbers. All of this paints a very bleak picture. Nevertheless, success can be had on rainy days, if the falconer ways up flights very carefully. Also, until a suitable chance arises, he must keep his eagle as dry as possible. Here, of course, the hood is a tremendous help. The calm, hooded eagle is less affected by the rain than the bating, restless, unhooded bird.

When hawking near home, bad weather can be worked around, and schedules are simply altered. This is not the case if one is invited for a day's hawking and plans have been laid weeks in advance. In such an instance it is a case of trying to make the most of a bad situation. This is exactly what I found myself doing on a day in early December, 1994. At the time I was living at Burg Hohenwerfen in Austria's Salzburger Land, this being the base for the center Hiebeler had been planning in 1993.

Located in a mountainous region, Hohenwerfen put me on the doorstep of high, rugged country. It was exciting terrain to be in but the price was a heavy work load. The beginning of the hawking season had been full of frustration with flying display commitments and other work eating into hunting time. Sick to death of hearing how good this or that meeting had been, as the weather cooled I

94

decided to make the most of every single hawking opportunity. Such a chance came up in the form of an invitation from Alois Emminger. He organized private hawking days for a small falcony group in Upper Austria. I had been a guest of his a few weeks earlier and with the marvelous weather conditions and plenty of quarry the sport had been excellent. It had been quite a drive but the two hares I came home with made the trip worthwhile.

It was with this last visit in mind that I prepared for the coming meeting. With just a few days to go the weather had been absolutely perfect, hard frosts and clear skies. I love hawking under such conditions and Astur too was alert and eager to hunt. His flying had been faultless, both at home and away, and as I loaded him into the car on the morning of the meeting I wondered what the day would bring.

On the road the skies promised another cold day and I could visualize crisp conditions at my destination. However, my optomistic frame of mind was soon to be shaken. I was just half an hour into my journey when the skies began to cloud over. The further I went the darker it became. Then the rain started and stayed with me nearly all the way there. But there was a glimmer of hope. As I neared the village where we were meeting the rain actually ceased.

Our base for the day's hawking was a small guest house and in the garden conditions were not too wet to prevent me putting the bird out to get some air. I arrived just before midday and as I waited for Emminger and the other three expected eagle owners, I went inside for a coffee. But I hardly had the cup to my lips before the heavens opened again. Desperate to keep the eagle dry I rushed out and put him back in his transport box. The other members of the group were soon to arrive and we decided to wait to see if the rain would pass. But staring out of the guest house window it was only too obvious that the drizzle and mist was in for the day. As we sat chatting the rain became harder than ever but, with no other option, at one o'clock it was decided to get out, even if for just an hour.

The hunting area was within walking distance and we soon found ourselves lined up and ready to commence the hunt. The group contained three male eagles and two females. One of the females, an immature bird, was being flown by a falconer from a rival center, and, of course, neither of us wanted to let our respective sides down. Emminger, himself, was flying an immature male and it was this bird that had the first flight. He was unsuccessful.

The area we were flying over had held a huge number of hares the previous year but on the day in question we were seeing very few. Those that were seen were quickly challenged and as we finished the first area allocated to us, every bird in the group, except Astur, had been flown. Not one hare had been put up at anything like a flyable distance from me. Also we had been walking through a lot of saturated cover and, I have to admit, I would have scrutinized even a reasonable slip very carefully indeed. I was only too aware that I needed to make every single flight count. Clear ground was coming up and it was here I hoped to be successful.

It was something of a surprise to see that I was the only person flying out of the hood. This was working to my advantage. The eagle had not budged once and was remarkably dry. Naturally, his primary and tail tips were wet where water had run onto them but generally his folded wings and tail, protected as they were, had remained unaffected. Still I waited and as I did, more unsuccessful flights were experienced by the other birds. Some of these flights resulted in the eagles going into trees, and as they brushed against moisture laden branches their plumage was rendered less effective than ever. My seemingly relaxed approach had two nearby beaters baffled. To them I must have appeared a little peculiar and, inexperienced as they were, my use of the hood mystified them. Indeed, their whispered comments revealed that they had given up on me doing anything at all.

By this time we had been out about fifty minutes and during this period the weather had become increasingly better. The rain that had greeted us as we left the guest house had become a light drizzle, and then had finally stopped. I had removed Astur's hood once or twice to keep his mind on the business at hand and everything about the way he rode on the glove told me that he was ready to do his part. Then our chance came. We were walking a ploughed field which, despite the weather, was quite dry. Here a squatting hare was located.

osef Hiebeler (center) and the author (left) at the Opocno meeting in 1992. *Photo: T. Large*

A familiar scene at a European falconry meeting.   *Photo: T. Dollmar*

Group hawking: a mistake is made and two eagles come together on a kill.   *Photo: T. Dollma*

Russian falconer with a female eagle. This bird is being carried on a lightweight T-perch.

Photo: T. Dollmann

Opposite page: High cover in Hungary.   *Photo: T. Dollmann*

Top: Rewarding an eagle at the scene of a kill.   *Photo: T. Dollmann*

Left: Kazakhstan: Machan with his fox catching eagle.

Photo: A. Zechmeister

Bottom: Hunting flight over heavy cover.   *Photo: T. Dollmann*

This interesting shot requires some explanation. A hare has just been missed in cover and the eagle has been quickly scooped up and thrown skyward as another hare flushes. The tactic worked and the bird went on to catch the hare.   *Photo: T. Anderle*

Below: Close to the action.   *Photo: L. Uhlir*

Relaxing for a few minutes.

Photo: T. Etheridge

Eagle with hare.

Photo: T. Dollmann

Cleaning a female
eagle's feet.
Photos: J. Hiebeler

Cleaning a female
eagle's feet—close up

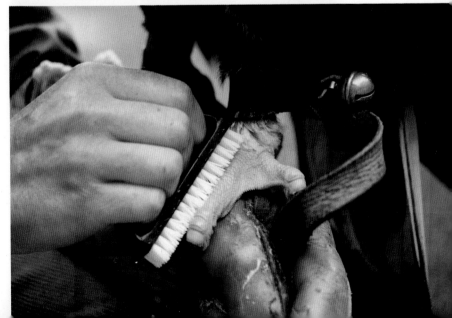

Straightening tail and
wing tips.

Photos: J. Hiebeler

Straightening tail and
wing tips—close up.

Head study of female eagle.

Photo: Autho

The quarry taken at an international meeting in Hungary.   Photo: T. Dollmann

A small hawking meet in Upper Austria, 1994.

Photo: R. Emminger

hare flushes close to the vehicles at a field meeting.

Photo: T. Dollmann

Kazakhstan: an impressive backdrop.
Photo: A. Zechmeister

The author in high country.
Photo: T. Etheridge

Young golden eagles.
Photo: Author

Male eagle feeding in the presence of two well-mannered dogs.
Photo: Author

Opposite page top: Lure training with the aid of a horse—shot one. *Photo: A. Zechmeister*

Opposite page middle: Lure training with the aid of a horse—shot two. *Photo: A. Zechmeister*

Opposite page bottom: Lure training with the aid of a horse—shot three. *Photo: A. Zechmeister*

ure training with the aid of a horse—shot four. *Photo: A. Zechmeister*

Acceptance and mutual respect. Jürgen Färber with an abnormally colored male eagle.

Photo: U. Rei<

Off to my right, it had been spotted by one of the beaters. Invisible to me, I was told that the hare was facing in my direction and so making a massive detour I tried to get behind the hiding animal. Still, I could see nothing, but as I tentatively eased into position, my right hand remained ready to grab for the hood. With no cover nearby, this was a flight to make the most of and with this in mind I gave the hare plenty of room. Then removing Astur's hood I gave him a second to orientate himself and with a hand gently held against his breast, I asked the beater to flush the quarry. A handful of soil was thrown and with the eagle standing tall, the hare exploded from its form.

From the directions I had been given I expected to be directly behind the target, but this was not the case. I was in fact slightly off to the left. Nevertheless, due to my distance, this fact alone did not worry me at all. More of a nuisance was that a group of spectators were now less than ideally positioned and the hare on seeing or sensing them, almost reversed its direction completely and headed off at speed on a tightly curving escape route. If I had been a few meters closer the flight would have been lost, and as I watched Astur struggle to follow the hare's path, I held my breath. It was a difficult maneuver he needed to perform and as his huge wings fought to keep him on line it seemed he would lose the speed he required. So demanding was this flight that it looked as if the hare really would leave its pursuer behind. It was now that the bird's dogged determination was most obvious, refusing to be beaten, he simply would not give in. Yet right up until the final stages of the flight it appeared his efforts would be in vain. Then suddenly it was over. One moment the hare was running, the next it was in the eagle's feet. Here the quarry was held until I was able to dispatch it. What a fine hare it was and fur strewn about the scene of the kill was evidence of the struggle it had put up.

After the taking of this hare I inspected Astur carefully. His plumage was certainly dirty but he was not particularly wet and with the rain still holding off I knew he would be able and willing to hunt on. My colleagues sadly had other ideas. With no quarry being taken by their eagles and all of them now really too wet to fly, they wanted to bring the day to a close. I was a little disappointed at their decision but consoled myself with the fact that Astur had provided a nice, big hare for the larder.

The Use of Dogs

A good dog can be a terrific asset to the hare hawker, especially if he frequently finds himself without human assistance. Indeed, at times a dog is almost essential. When hares are sitting tight in areas of extensive cover, they can be extremely difficult to find without canine help. What one requires is a dog that points hares, rather than finds and flushes them. The pointing dog gives the falconer time to prepare and position himself for the slip.

I find the pleasure I derive from hawking hares is greatly increased when a sensible dog is making up part of the team, the dog work itself adding an additional exciting element. There is something captivating about watching a dog steadily work the field ahead, knowing that at any moment it might come on point; and when the point does finally come, I often find myself quite tense with anticipation.

It is often thought that eagles and dogs cannot be safely worked together, but this is not so. If the eagle in question has been introduced to dogs correctly, it will not be a constant threat to its four-footed ally. Nevertheless, it would certainly be very unwise to take a sharp hunting eagle into an area where it might encounter strange dogs. Care, too, must be taken when flying over a dog the eagle does not know particularly well; for example, if flying out of the hood, make sure eagle and dog have ample time to inspect each other before commencing the hunt. In an effort to avoid problems, it is also worth considering the dog's color. A distinctively marked or light-colored dog is easily discernible in cover and less likely to be confused with quarry by the eagle. Larger dogs are obviously preferable to smaller ones.

As invaluable as canine assistance can be, when a flight opportunity is lost, the poor dog is often blamed. However, so very often the fault can actually lie with the falconer himself. Let me explain how, on one occasion, I proved to be the guilty party. Three of us decided to try to grab a couple of hours of hawking one wintry

114

afternoon. The area we had targeted was a slightly elevated, flat-topped expanse of treeless, agricultural ground, little more than fifteen minutes drive from base. The eagle we had with us was Astur. In addition, we had an English setter along. Dog and eagle knew each other well and were quite safe to work together.

The spot we decided to work was a section of dead, spindly vegetation. This was quite tall, in places almost waist height, but sparse enough to make off-the-fist flights viable. The whole patch was laid out in one wide, long strip. Had we not had the dog, we would have needed either more human beaters or been faced with working the cover in two sections. With the setter to help us, we were fairly confident of being able to hunt through this crop in one sweep.

Although the landscape itself was fairly even, on one side of the cover strip, the ground eased away slightly uphill. Our chosen direction put this bank on my right and it was a little way up this bank and out of the cover that I positioned myself. To my left, walking the strip, were my two colleagues and working with them, the dog.

Our pace was steady and slow and my eyes were fixed firmly on the setter, as she searched sensibly and thoroughly. This was a dog I liked very much, easy to control in the field, gentle and kind-natured. She belonged to one of my companions, who used her primarily for hawking feathered quarries with falcons, but she would also point hares, hence her presence on this particular day. We had witnessed one or two "possibles," occasions when it seemed the dog might have located a hare and each time my right hand hovered over the eagle's hood. Then the dog came on what I believed to be a definite point and at that exact same moment a shout went up, "Hare, hare!" All I could think was, "where, where?" My eyes were still firmly on the dog (who was some way ahead of her handler) and I assumed that, somewhere out in front of her, a hare was up and running. But strain as I did, I could not for the life of me see a thing. Again, "Hare, hare!"

This was too much: with no quarry ahead of me or the dog, I quickly unhooded the eagle and was amazed when he veered off sharply to the left and toward my assistants, who were a little way behind me. A hare had been put up right from under their feet. This hare was now running left, but moving at no great speed. Its lack of haste may have been due to the fact that ahead of it lay an overgrown drainage ditch, and, with this sanctuary in sight, perhaps it did not feel too threatened. But the hare, unaware of the eagle, had put its life in jeopardy. Sweeping straight past my helpers, almost clipping one with a wing, Astur made up the distance very quickly indeed. However, with the ditch just a few meters away, it was going to be close. I was hoping that he would reach and tackle the hare before it made the ditch, but here I was unlucky. As the hare skipped into the cover and momentarily disappeared, the eagle made an attempt to take it. He was unsuccessful. A distance of less than a meter and a conveniently placed patch of thick undergrowth had saved the hare's skin, and, now feeling most definitely threatened, the lucky animal took to its heels across the ploughed field beyond. Had I been a bit more aware of what was going on, the hare might not have been so fortunate.

Eagle Versus Hawk and Buteo

Because several smaller hunting birds are capable of taking brown hares, the hare hawker's need for a golden eagle is sometimes questioned. However, although female goshawks, Harris' hawks and red-tailed hawks will account for hares, none of these will match the performance of a well-flown golden eagle. Here, of course, one has to differentiate between taking a small number of hares and a more concentrated effort.

If one disregards hunting styles, it must be acknowledged that flights to brown hares, especially on hard ground, can be very punishing. Even if mentally prepared, the smaller hawks are just not designed to repeatedly absorb the abuse that this kind of hawking deals out. An adult hare is a muscular power house. Once captured, this power, much of it directed to the back legs, will combine with the hare's body weight to give the small- or medium-sized bird an experience it will not soon forget. In some encounters, the hawk will simply be kicked off, leaving the hare to continue on its way, but in others, things can get very rough indeed. These more physical confrontations are no mere skirmishes in the dirt. They can see hawk and hare leave the ground completely only to come crashing back to earth in a confusion of fur and feathers.

I recall reading an interesting hare hawking article written by two North American falconers. They had spent a season hawking brown hares with ferruginous hawks in Ontario. They experienced some success, but noted just how tough this quarry was for even a big female ferruginous. The article finished with them inviting any interested fellow falconers out for a day's hawking, but suggested that such an outing be left until near the end of the season. This advice was offered because it was felt that, after getting to grips with a few brown hares, their visitors' birds probably would not be fit for anything else until the following season!

In the search for a bird suited to their needs, a number of hare hawkers (like those in Ontario) have looked to the ferruginous hawk. This North American badlands buteo is an admirable species and its weight, power and rather specialized nature certainly indicates that it needs to be separated, from a falconry point of view, from the smaller, more frequently utilized birds. Some falconers would place the potent ferruginous hawk nearer to the golden eagle, but to actually compare the two as hunting hawks in the field is quite wrong. As trained birds, eagle and buteo are very different to work with. Putting aside, for a moment, actual hare-catching ability, one has to recognize that the ferruginous is quite a unique raptor and is geared to function under fairly specific conditions. This is a bird of open plains and prairie-type landscapes, and, if removed from its natural environment, its potential as a falconry bird is limited. Unlike the golden eagle, it will not hunt in woodland and is even incompatible with semi-open terrain; and this reluctance to fly in timbered habitats or even use trees as perches makes hawking in anything but spacious, unrestricted country totally impractical.

If one accepts the ferruginous for the open country specialist it is, then this raptor has true potential as a hare hawk. It is swift, powerful, and, once entered to quarry, extremely determined. Nevertheless, when it comes to hunting the very largest hares, a female ferruginous is not, in my opinion, in the same class as a golden eagle. This has nothing to do with any lack of willingness on the buteo's part to tackle hares; this it will do and with commitment. It has more to do with the bird's build. For its size, the ferruginous does not possess very big feet. Its feet are certainly strong and the toes stout, but the actual span of the foot is surprisingly small for a bird that regularly takes hares in the wild. However, this species' ability to catch hares should not be allowed to overshadow the fact that, during the summer months, it preys heavily on smaller, less demanding mammals (for example, ground squirrels), and, for securing relatively small-bodied prey, the ferruginous has feet of quite an appropriate size.

A smallish foot span does not prevent the ferruginous from catching hares as a trained hunting hawk, but it does not help it control its victims once it actually hits them. A female ferruginous is definitely capable of taking adult brown hares and the flights can be long and thrilling, but a golden eagle will give a very much stronger performance against this quarry. One only has to examine the eagle's impressively sized and heavily armed feet to see that it is simply far better equipped for the job. Then there is the eagle's great physical strength and durability. All in all, with this raptor, one has a hare hawk without equal.

The Mountain Hare, Prairie Hare and Sage Brush Hare

So far, this chapter has concerned itself with the brown hare. At this point, I would like to widen things slightly to mention three other species, beginning with the mountain hare. This lagomorph is found throughout the northern Palaearctic region in tundra and boreal forest habitats. It is encountered in the tundra zone of North America and there is a somewhat isolated population in the European Alps. The mountain hare is indigenous to Scotland and Ireland.

The mountain hare is known by a variety of names. In North America, it is referred to as the arctic hare, and, in Scotland, a commonly used name is blue hare. Its size varies, depending on the particular sub-species and where it is found. For example, the mountain hare of Scotland is a smaller animal than its Irish counterpart. Probably the most noticeable feature about this hare is its habit of moulting into a white or whitish winter coat (though not all mountain hares turn completely white in winter). In the most northerly regions, this white coat is kept all year round.

In Scotland, the mountain hare is an animal associated with high ground, tending to remain above an altitude of approximately 375 meters (however, at times, it will be encountered lower than this). The preferred habitat is heather moorland and rough pasture. In north-eastern Scotland, the management of grouse moors creates an ideal environment for mountain hares and here they thrive.

Being a smaller animal than the brown hare, the Scottish mountain hare has been pursued by falconers flying a variety of raptors. Of course, much of the pleasure derived from hawking this hare comes from the breath-taking country one can find oneself in. The terrain is often well suited to soaring flights and these have been enjoyed by Harris' hawk, buteo and eagle owners. This hare may not be enormous, but with a weight of approximately 2.3 to 3 kg, it is still a more than fitting (and indeed, natural) quarry for golden eagles; and what could be more dramatic than the sight of an eagle soaring against the backdrop of the high, wild country that this lagomorph inhabits?

Moving on, in North America, two regularly hunted falconry quarries are the prairie hare and the sage brush hare. Both of these hares can be taken with birds smaller than a golden eagle, but the eagle owner should certainly place them high on his list of possible quarries. The prairie hare or white-tailed jackrabbit deserves special consideration. This is the larger of the two and resembles the brown hare in size. It has a more northerly range than the sage brush hare and is found on the northern plains and across the Canadian prairies. This hare is a very fast animal and it has been stated that, of North American mammals, only the pronghorn antelope can match or better its speed. To complement this speed is staying power. Like the brown hare, the prairie hare possesses terrific stamina. This may not be obvious to the falconer (who never fully tests this capability), but any hunter who has pursued this quarry with sight hounds will testify as to just how much of an endurance runner the prairie hare is.

The sage brush hare or black-tailed jackrabbit has a wide distribution across western North America, south to Mexico. This is a hare of desert and grassland environments. It will be found on the perimeter of agricultural areas and will use these; however, it does not do well where the land is given over entirely to agricultural development. This desert lagomorph may not be able to quite match the staggering speed of the prairie hare, but it makes up for this with its superior agility. It is this agility and the evasive tactics this hare employs, that makes it so appealing to the ground quarry enthusiast.

Dispatching Hares

Although hares are not as large as some eagle quarries, I would still strongly advise running to lend assistance. Once on the scene a variety of methods can be employed to dispatch the victim. Using a knife at the animal's head is a very effective approach, but the blade should have no cutting edge for a mistake can result in the bird's feet being injured. With this risk in mind I have even used a large bradawl. For those unfamiliar with this instrument it resembles a pointed screwdriver.

Another option is to apply hard pressure to the hare's chest. This can be done in several ways. A clenched fist can be used. When this is the case the action is not a punch. Instead a hard push is applied and held. The falconer's knee can also be used in this fashion.

7 Hare Hawking in Group Situations

When golden eagle owners assemble for a day's sport in Europe, they will normally have brown hares in mind. Pursuing hares as part of a group differs significantly from the private hare-hawking experience, and, although such get-togethers can be extremely enjoyable, they do require the falconer to exercise more caution and restraint than when flying alone. In a group hawking situation, everyone's first concern should be safety; and the desire to take quarry should never see any falconer deliberately put another person's eagle at risk. Confrontations involving two or more eagles are to be avoided at all costs, and, here, one also has to try to think for the other person, never taking anything for granted. Of course, if one is hawking in familiar company, the safety of all the birds involved is easier to guarantee. However, even then, mistakes do occur and accidents can happen, and, because of this, the falconer should not allow himself to be lulled into a false sense of security.

The risk of birds coming together on quarry can never be fully ruled out; it is something that does occasionally happen. But the risks can be reduced and the individual falconer can do a lot to try to ensure the safety of his bird, as well as those belonging to other participants. First of all, he will need to be aware of the various rules that are employed in group hawking situations. To highlight these, I will need to describe just what form the hawking itself takes and how things actually proceed once the party is assembled in the field.

On arriving at the hawking area, falconers will form a line facing the terrain to be flown over. How long this line is will depend on the number of eagles and the number of spectators-*cum*-beaters on hand. A good number of beaters is always a great asset, for it means that eagle owners can be kept well apart without leaving huge gaps in the line; and, when walking across areas of low ground cover where hares are tempted to sit tight, the smaller the gaps, the better.

The hawking itself is reasonably straightforward. The group moves off across country, keeping the line as straight as possible and walking at a fairly slow pace. Any hares that flush will be flown at by whichever falconer is nearest to them. In practice, this means that each eagle owner has a corridor of ground ahead of him that is "his," and any hares getting up too far to the left or right should not be slipped at, these then being in the next falconer's area. This is perhaps the first and most basic group hawking rule, but even here genuine mistakes can occur, especially with hares that are flushed on the "border" going left or right. Because of this, I would advise the falconer who can guarantee his own self-control and judgment to pick his position in the hawking line very carefully. Naturally, one will wish to avoid any falconer who has a reputation for flying dangerously. Being next to someone like this can spoil a day completely, for one is simply too nervous to fly at all. In addition, I have a policy regarding female eagles. If I am flying a male, I try to keep away from them. The reason for this is very simple. If two male eagles grab hold of the same hare, the outcome may not be serious at all, particularly if they can be reached quickly. But if a squabble should develop and a female eagle is involved, then a male can receive crippling injuries. I can think of several male eagles that have had their careers cut short by large females.

If possible, I try to acquire the first or final position in the hawking line. This results in me having only one side to concern myself about. I say "try" because at formal meetings positions will be allocated at the group leader's discretion. He will tend to pace the line out, asking falconers to remain where he places them. But even then, a little negotiating is often possible. With an end of line place secured, one really needs a couple of beaters to provide coverage on the open side. If this type of hare-flushing help can be obtained, one has a truly favorable position. That said, I would most definitely avoid a flank position if this placed me within eagle range of a road or, worse still, power lines. I hate to think how many trained eagles have been killed on high voltage power lines. The problem is that, in very open, flat country, electricity masts represent the only elevated perching places, and, after an unsuccessful flight, an eagle can so easily be tempted to swing up onto one of these deadly masts.

To return to the business of slipping, if a hare is flown at by one of the group, the other members should halt. They will need to remain stationary until the loose eagle has either been retrieved or, if successful, taken up from its kill. If the line proceeds, then a second hare might be flushed and flown at and there will be another eagle free. Now, if this second eagle misses its hare, it might very well try to get to the first eagle as it sits on its kill. Or, if the first eagle was unsuccessful, but has remained at liberty, it could prove to be a danger to the second bird if this makes contact with quarry.

At times, playing safe can be a frustrating game. How well I remember a field meeting that found my guests and I having to deal with an almost unbearable situation. I had been joined in the field by a French sporting journalist and her photographer and also an English guest. We were at a large meeting in eastern Europe and my companions felt they might get more out of the day latching onto an English-speaking falconer.

By midday, we had experienced no success and with my guests relying on me to provide some action, I was starting to feel a little warm under the collar. At length, we found ourselves overlooking a large, rough field of broken earth. Baked hard by the sun, this treacherous, uneven terrain was not the type of surface to cross in a carefree manner. We had become somewhat separated from the main party, which was now further over to the left and the only other eagle in our mini-group was a very large female. I was only too aware of her size due to the fact that my own bird was a male and probably the smallest golden eagle I had ever flown; he was also rather inexperienced. The area was dotted with small, stumpy trees and it was into one of these, following an unsuccessful flight, that the female eagle went. Although her location put her some distance from my guests and I, the elevated perch she occupied gave her a commanding view of the field. To proceed would have been foolish. Unfortunately, the errant eagle was most reluctant to return to her owner, who was eventually seen employing all manner of tricks in an effort to tempt her down. But still she would not budge.

It was at this point that, off to the left, I noticed a lone spectator making his way across the rough ground ahead of us. I could hardly believe my bad luck when he flushed one, two, then three hares. All of these came within slipping distance of us, and, with the brutally rough ground balancing the odds, even my inexperienced bird would have been in with a real chance. But the situation was hopeless. On that bare, open field, my little male would have been an easy target for the tree-sitting female eagle.

My reluctance to fly totally baffled those around me—why was "our" eagle not in pursuit? I quickly explained to my guests that although the female eagle was perched motionless on her branch (and had either not seen the hares or had simply chosen not to respond), the sight of another eagle making a kill would almost certainly bring her back to life. I was not prepared to take such a risk. However, our disappointment was short-lived. On the very next field, I located a squatting hare, and, with no obstructions (and the female eagle now secured), the photographer got his action shots and the eagle his hare.

Having two eagles free in different parts of the field only becomes a serious matter if one of them actually takes quarry. If both of them fail to make contact with their individual hares, no problems will arise; and the same would apply if both were successful. But who can guarantee such things? No, on the whole, it really is wise to observe the "one hare, one eagle" rule. There is perhaps a possible exception, an instance where a falconer might be forgiven for slipping a second eagle. It sometimes happens that a hare will be flown at and either refused or missed by one eagle, only to have its escape route bring it very close to another falconer. Such a hare, out on its own and not being pursued, can prove very tempting, indeed. However, assessing the risk in such a situation takes skill. The hare will need to be very close and the original, now grounded eagle, will need to be a considerable distance away. Just because the grounded eagle has made no attempt to follow "its" hare, it should not be assumed that it will not wish to get involved if another eagle takes this hare. Here, just how the original eagle behaves will be influenced by first, its distance from the second eagle (now in possession of the hare); second, whether or not it can actually see this bird (eagle and quarry may be hidden); and third, how near it is to its owner and how quickly he intervenes (that is, attracts its attention with food or actually retrieves it). The alert falconer who sees by his bird's reactions that it is about to try to reach the other eagle will get to it as fast as possible, all the time displaying food on the glove. But when all is said and done, the falconer flying the second eagle has one calculation to make that overrides everything else. If things go wrong, could he get to his own bird (if it takes quarry) well before eagle number one arrives on the scene? Yet, even with this decision, there are problems, for, once the eagle has left the glove, it is impossible to predict with total accuracy how any flight might unfold. The wind direction and landscape will need to be considered and it should be remembered that a short slip does not necessarily mean a short flight.

Personally, with this type of thing, I would be looking for a hare coming almost past me, after being missed at the other end of the hawking line. Let me give an account of just such a follow-up flight. A group of us were hawking hares across open ground. My own position placed me at the far right-hand side of the line, with perhaps four eagles and several beaters stretching off to the left. A hare was flushed and attempted by a friend's eagle on the far left. This bird powered in, but was unsuccessful. The hare, already swinging right, was forced to alter its route and now was running almost parallel to the line. No other falconer made any attempt to fly it, and, with the unsuccessful eagle still grounded, I seized the chance and slipped my eagle. To the right of me was an area of marshy ground containing tall reeds and coarse grass. It was for this that the panicked hare was now heading and I was quite sure that the flight would finish here.

The hare would either be caught or lost. This made the flight far safer than it might otherwise have been, especially as the spot was easily within my reach. Into the undergrowth went the hare and over the top went the eagle. As calculated, there was no lengthy pursuit: almost immediately the eagle tipped over and went in for the kill. A splash was heard, and, within moments, I was on the scene. The eagle had taken the hare in a water-filled depression. I dispatched the quarry swiftly, and, making sure that the first eagle had been secured (it had never been very far from its owner), I carefully removed my eagle from its kill. The capture of this particularly large hare was not fully appreciated by my colleague who had originally flown at it. He insisted that the hare had only been caught because it had "stumbled into a ditch!"

If employed at all, this type of flying is best reserved for when one is hunting in familiar company and with familiar birds. It is not something to attempt if the group contains one or two eagles that are known to be aggressive with others; and let me emphasize that it is definitely not a type of flying simply to be adopted by the individual as part of his group hawking strategy.

It is worth noting that, when a very large eagle group is assembled, slipping rules are sometimes eased a little to account for hares flushing in different parts of a very long line; and, when well-spaced hares flush simultaneously, one will invariably see two or perhaps even three eagles on the wing. Nevertheless, no experienced falconer would ever deliberately slip an eagle while another bird was actually down on quarry.

Whether precautions are taken or not, sooner or later the eagle owner is going to find himself in a difficult two-bird situation. For example, let us imagine that, while a falconer is attending his eagle at the scene of a kill, a shout alerts him to the presence of another loose and on-coming eagle. On his own and without any assistance, he has very few choices. With his bird at risk, the safest plan of action is to take up his bird and move away, leaving the kill for the approaching eagle. Here, quick thinking can prevent a potentially dangerous situation from arising.

Because problems can occur even when hawking in very experienced company, I would strongly advise against including eagles in hawking groups containing smaller raptors. The danger here lies not only in the fact that hawk and eagle might be slipped accidentally at the same quarry or clash in some similar way, but also that a hawk might be at risk even when on its owner's fist. It should never be assumed that, just because a particular eagle is "safe" with other eagles, it will be safe with hawks or buteos. An eagle returning to its trainer following an unsuccessful flight might very well be drawn to the flapping, erratic behavior of a small near-by hawk. Let there be no mistake about it: hawks have been killed in this way. Although mixed groups can work, I think most eagle owners would agree that, at meetings, eagles are far better off in their own special party.

Before leaving the topic of possible dangers, I would like to say a few words about feral cats, for if the falconer is foolish enough to fly at them, then these too represent a hazard. Feral cats are often encountered by hare hawking groups, and, when put up on open arable land, they can appear a very tempting target indeed. Possessing none of the hare's speed and maneuverability, a feral cat might seem to present the less successful falconer with an opportunity to finally put something in the bag. However, although the flight itself should not be too demanding, subduing and holding the victim can prove a very different matter. The domestic cat, turned self-sufficient, lowland hunter, is a formidable adversary and is capable of seriously injuring an eagle. What makes cats so lethal is the weaponry they possess. Not only does the eagle have sharp, biting teeth to contend with (as it does with foxes), it is also faced with flailing legs armed with scimitar-like claws. Feral cats can be taken with trained eagles, but for the amount of sport involved, it seems madness to risk a valued bird.

Moving on, there are still a couple of field procedures to be discussed that, although not designed to prevent accidents, are important. The main one I would draw attention to is the "rule" concerning retrieving birds in the field. If an eagle has had an unsuccessful flight, it should be called back to the fist with as little fuss as possible. If the eagle will not return and its owner must fetch, or at least move closer to it, then he must exercise a little thought and consideration when doing so. First, the falconer should try to walk the same route the fleeing hare took, thereby disturbing less fresh ground. Secondly, once he is in possession of his eagle, he should stay where he is and wait for the group to reach him. During this waiting period, he should not attempt to fly at any hares flushed by the group as they walk toward him. The reason for him needing to remain stationary is fairly obvious. Any moving about or any attempt made to walk back to the group might result in hares being inadvertently flushed. This type of thing always needs to be borne in mind when an eagle has to be retrieved. If a bird ends up on the far left or far right of the hawking party, it is often advisable to walk straight down the hawking line. This allows the hawking area in front to be avoided completely.

Another bit of group hawking etiquette that needs to be mentioned concerns flying at quarry. Accepting that group situations tend to generate an air of friendly competition and that each falconer naturally wishes to see his bird do well, there is still room for a little consideration. For example, any falconer who has already enjoyed his fair share of success should think for a moment before flying at any squatting hare he finds. In some cases, it is far more sporting to offer such a prize opportunity to a less successful falconer and especially if this person is flying a first-year bird. Naturally, one has to use a little common sense. A falconer some way off in the distance cannot be helped, but should nearby neighbors qualify, one can easily alert them to the presence of a "squatter" and even (if one's own bird is hooded) flush it for them.

Actually accounting for quarry in a large golden eagle group can be a difficult business for those more used to hawking alone. Even falconers who commonly hunt in group set-ups will often feel under pressure when trying to function in a big eagle party, containing perhaps ten or twelve birds. Taking quarry relies very much on assessing situations quickly and accurately and this is a basic requirement for successful hare hawking. However, luck also plays a part (and frequently a very big part) in just how many flights one gets. Hares will not be spread evenly and "fairly" over the land ahead of the party and one section of the line might easily find itself walking better hare ground than another. This can influence things quite dramatically. Indeed, at a recent three-day meeting, I had hardly any flights on the first day and no quarry at all, but on the second day saw plenty of action and took four hares. Of course, one's fortunes can change during the course of a day. Even on flat, agricultural land, ground conditions will be constantly changing and so, too, will hare densities. Long periods can pass without much happening at all, then suddenly hares seem to be everywhere!

In an effort to make the most out of any opportunities that do arise, it is well worth making sure that the falconers on either side of one's own position are actually flying their birds. This may sound a little strange, but it can be that, after taking one or two hares, a falconer may decide either to finish hawking for the day or perhaps just for a period of time. If this happens, one can fully exploit the situation. Nevertheless, it still pays to periodically check how things stand. It is strange how a bird that is not due to be flown can quickly be on the wing if a fox jumps up in front of its owner!

Flight chances often materialize late in the day when most of the group may consider the outing to be as good as over. This lack of concentration can work to the advantage of any party member who keeps alert right through the closing stages of the hunt. I have taken many hares in this way and I cannot resist mentioning one of these flights here. This flight remains vivid and separate from countless others because it was experienced at a large Czechoslovakian hawking meet and the hare was almost "stolen" from under the noses of fellow falconers. But before the selected flight, perhaps I should set the scene with a little background about the meeting itself. Heading the get-together was Ivan Marosi; indeed, it was at this mid-1980s assembly that he and I first met. He was flying a female goshawk and his field performance was as respectable as the position he held. One hare he accounted for was so large that it made him the envy of several eagle owners.

A variety of birds had been brought along, but for hawking purposes, they were divided into groups (the eagles having two groups to themselves). The surrounding countryside offered suitable flying conditions for falcons, goshawks and eagles, each group being guided to an appropriate area. The part of Czechoslovakia we were in is known today as Slovakia, after becoming separated from the now Czech Republic in 1993. The northern half of Slovakia is dominated by the Tatra mountains; the meeting, however, was located further south on the agricultural ground that forms a plain drained by the river Danube. Technically, Slovakia (like the Czech republic) is a central European country, but to me this will always be part of eastern Europe. My thinking stems from the fact that I first came to know this area when it belonged to the Eastern Block. Then, one had a definite feeling of traveling from west to east. The lure was the guarantee of sport and action, and, in the past, Czechoslovakia has seen hare hawking on a truly incomparable scale.

With over a dozen eagles present, this particular meet had attracted a good number of hare-orientated falconers and all were keen to take advantage of the opportunity they were now presented with. Hares were abundant, but I must say that some of the flying was, to put it mildly, a little inconsiderate. On the first day (there were three actual hawking days), Maroši led the eagle group I was in and, during one of his own flights, had no less than three eagles in the air behind his goshawk! Luckily, the hawk failed to get to the hare it was pursuing; otherwise the outcome would have been fairly certain. I also had a heart-stopping moment. After a particularly dangerous female eagle had been pointed out to me, I watched in horror as this bird was late slipped behind my own. My male eagle missed its hare and landed, but the female caught a bit of wind and, for a moment or two, held her position right over him. The female's owner quickly called her to a rabbit's leg held in his hand and she responded. My own bird remained motionless throughout, staring in the direction of his escaped hare.

But now to proceed to the late day flight I wanted to describe. It took place on the second day of the meet. It had been a long day and I had not seen a great deal of sport. Much of this was perhaps my own fault as I had been flying very cautiously (and who could blame me!). Even so, I had accounted for one hare quite early on and knew, if the right opportunity came along, I would certainly be in with a chance of taking another. That said, I must confess that, as we began the last section to be walked over, I wondered if I had been a little too reserved.

The rest of the group were somewhat bunched up and actually chatting amongst themselves and I found myself alone and quite a way off to their left. The day was bright, totally still and on the flat, bare plain ahead of us, nothing stirred. Then I saw it. A long-range hare was on the move, going straight away from the group in an unconcerned manner. I quickly glanced to my right to see if anybody else was about to slip, but engrossed in conversation, my colleagues had not seen the faraway target. This flight was all mine, and, as the eagle left the glove, I gave a precautionary shout, "Eagle free!" My companions were brought back to the hunt with a jolt and we stood motionless, intently watching the action. On the featureless land-scape, the hare, although some way off, looked extremely conspicu-ous. So too did the eagle as it closed the gap between itself and its intended victim.

That the slip had been a long one did not concern me greatly. The hare's "casual" attitude made the flight quite feasible. I also had a good deal of confidence in the bird itself. He possessed terrific straight line performance and I was relying on this to overwhelm the hare he had in his sights. At the beginning of the flight, the hare's distance had prompted one or two negative grunts. However, now with the eagle rapidly covering ground, the tone changed somewhat and one could feel the whole party urging him on. If the hare realized the peril it was in, then it realized too late. The eagle went in hard and a spontaneous cheer went up from the onlookers. With shouts of "Run, Englander, run!" echoing behind me, I began to sprint to-wards the scene of the kill. My long flight gamble had paid off, and, with the bagging of this final hare, the day came to a close.

When hunting in a large group, keeping up with how many hares are being taken is impossible. That birds are being flown and are making kills will be obvious, but with a huge chunk of the line sometimes very far away, just which falconers are having luck is often far from clear. This, I think gives an idea of how far some of these eagle lines can stretch. In open plains-type country, I have flown in groups so large that, from a flank position, the other end of the line just seemed to fade into the far distance.

Under such conditions, keeping up with a faraway colleague's progress is at best a hit and miss affair. A hand held high might be used to signal a possible result, but this kind of signaling seems primitive indeed when compared with the two-way radios used by one husband and wife team. From opposite ends of the field, information is passed back and forth not only about the type of sport being enjoyed, but any possible hazards. At times, it seems, a little strange, especially when hawking alongside one of them, but in many ways the radio idea is not such a bad one.

Just how much quarry ends up being taken during a day's hawking can be influenced greatly by the skill of the group leader. If officially appointed, he will have been chosen for his knowledge of the area, his hawking experience and his standing in the club. This makes him well qualified to lead the group and questioning the decisions he makes is not at all wise. Even when his tactics seem odd, for example, lining the group up to walk a rather unpromising piece of ground or facing the line into the wind, he should be given the benefit of the doubt (initially, anyway!). It must be remembered that only he knows the hawking area boundaries and those places that are to be avoided. Also, to reach really prime spots, the group will frequently need to walk large sections of less desirable ground. These points need to be borne in mind. If given a little room to maneuver, a good group leader will normally end up showing his party the flights they are looking for.

A rather undesirable set-up is when the hawking party is being led by someone with no personal falconry experience. This can easily happen when the party has been granted a day's hawking on a large estate, an estate where someone might have been laid on to guide the group. Even at some of the very large European meetings running over several days, it is not uncommon to find the group being guided through the various hunting areas by an individual who may never have seen a hunting bird in action. Such a person will normally come from a shooting background. He will know the area intimately and have a good idea where hares are likely to be found, but he will not be familiar with how a group carrying birds instead of guns operates. Sometimes a little guidance is required, and, when needed, this should be given very tactfully indeed and come from one of the group's more senior members.

Tact can be very difficult to guarantee if the group is obviously having obstacles placed in its way. It is quite possible to find one's party being led by a guide who is plainly anxious about too many hares being caught. This is quite understandable where hares are not particularly abundant; and no experienced falconer would want to over-hunt a sensitive area. Or, of course, it might be that hares are being reserved for shooting guests. In such cases, the group will normally be told just how many hares they can account for. When this number is reached, hawking ceases. However, less above-board tactics are sometimes employed by those keen to see as few hares as possible taken. These include insisting on lengthy discussions before heading out into the fields (this can work exceptionally well if the meeting place is an establishment where food and refreshments are available!) and arranging the parking place for the vehicles a very long way from the actual hawking area. The average eagle owner is fit—he has to be—and a long walk before the hunt is no major inconvenience. Even so, this obvious time-wasting ploy is aggravating and also totally unnecessary. Most owners would prefer to have a short, active spell in the field, rather than a long deliberately drawn-out day.

Finally, I would advise any falconer who finds himself in a group hawking situation to double check just what can be flown at. The group may be out looking for hares, but it is quite likely that other possible quarries will be flushed. Here, I am thinking primarily of roe deer and it is well worth finding out whether or not they can be attempted. There will be no time for questions if an opportunity suddenly presents itself.

Official Meetings

After examining the practical side of group hare hawking and how to avoid problems, I would like to add something on large official meetings. It is not only in the field that a code of conduct needs to be observed and those attending a large meeting for the first time can find the experience a little daunting. This section will outline how a large meeting operates and give bits of advice along the way.

Generally speaking, the bigger European meetings allow for three day's practical hawking. However, with an additional day set aside for falconers to arrive and register, a meeting will officially run over four days. This can actually be extended to five if one considers that most falconers will not head for home at the end of the final hawking day. The majority will give themselves time to unwind and leave the following day. Also, at the end of a large international meeting, there is normally a rather festive evening and this is something most participating falconers would not wish to miss.

Personally, I feel that the earlier one can arrive on the first day, the better. This way, one gets to choose the best spot at the weathering area and register before things become busy. Just what form the weathering area takes will depend on where the meeting is being held. It might simply be an area of lawn or take over a completely walled park. One thing is sure: some parts of the weathering area are going to be better than others and an early arrival ensures that a place in one of these spots can be reserved. Of paramount importance is that plenty of space is allowed between birds and it pays to repeatedly check this throughout the day (and meeting). One should never assume that another, late-arriving falconer will exercise the necessary degree of caution. Problems in this respect are few and far between, but better to be safe than sorry. It is also well worth inspecting the condition of the equipment others are using. Broken jesses, leashes and swivels can also lead to disaster. On the subject of equipment, it goes without saying that one should have a spare of everything along.

Regarding one's own attire, although there is no strict dress code, it would be inappropriate to wear anything too colorful or gaudy (hunting green being traditional). The idea is to harmonize with the setting and not contrast sharply with it; and, with a building such as the beautiful Schloss Opocno as a backdrop to the meet, a little respect is certainly called for. In addition to hunt gear, I would recommend packing a slightly more formal set of clothes for the final evening.

After settling one's eagle at the weathering area, the next stop should be the meeting's registration room. Here, fees will be paid, hunting license (if applicable) obtained and one will be given information regarding the accommodation. It is also here that the inquisitive falconer can normally discover just how many eagles are expected. A large number may indicate two eagle groups, but if just a few are attending, then only one party will be formed.

It is the people that really make these meetings. At an international gathering, a variety of countries will be represented and this creates a special atmosphere. This also tends to raise the question of language. English is, of course, a pretty good standby, but it would be wrong to assume that English will always suffice. To get the very most out of meetings in Hungary, the Czech Republic or Slovakia, a knowledge of German is indispensable; and here one must remember how popular these meetings are with German and Austrian falconers. I generally find myself speaking nothing but German. In fact, based as I invariably am for these meetings in Germany, or more recently Austria, I do not really see myself as a participating British falconer. At one meeting, someone even remarked, "You don't look very English!"

With registration and accommodation attended to, the most interesting place to be, in my opinion, is the weathering area. I like to park myself and observe the activity. As the day progresses, the scene becomes more and more lively. Falconers bustle back and forth unloading vehicles, inspecting other people's birds and generally whipping themselves up into a hunting fever. The picture may be a busy one, but there is still normally time for the odd hunting tale. Indeed, from a distance, some of these take on quite theatrical proportions as hands and arms are employed to describe a particular flight more graphically. Such performances involve both eagle and hawk owners and I should perhaps make it clear that these meetings are never devoted entirely to eagle flying. They generally attract many hawks and falcons, and, although eagle numbers can be high (the highest I have known was twenty-eight), these gatherings are not organized solely around eagles. At some meetings, one sees only a few eagles.

As things wind down at the weathering area, falconers will make their way to their rooms and then on to a favorite restaurant or guest house. At many meetings, one finds an almost campus-type arrangement, with everyone sleeping and eating under, near enough, one roof. When this is the case, the evenings can be true social events and the enthusiasm seen at the weathering area will be amplified with the aid of good beer and wine!

I find it difficult to capture on paper just what some of these evenings can be like. Of course, venues differ and the meeting's headquarters will dramatically influence the whole atmosphere. At some meetings, one can find quite a plush set-up; at others, things can be very basic. Oddly enough, the true hunter may well discover that some of the smaller, less publicized get-togethers have a more intense feel about them (due to reduced outside influence). But, whether large or small, all meetings have one thing in common: participating falconers will gather in the evenings to chat about a sport that binds them together so strongly. Glasses are scattered on tables, sitting around which are figures engrossed in discussion. A hand goes up and someone summons a colleague to assist with a translation and soon the proceedings are being conducted in three languages. Hurried sketches on bits of paper help ease the conversation along. In various parts of the room, similar scenes are to be witnessed. People are eating, drinking and talking, welcoming friends and sizing up the competition. A chair scrapes on the hard floor, a dog yelps and someone curses. Suddenly, the door swings open and in strides a familiar face. A flamboyant character, well known to all and his presence livens things up even more. Pulling up a chair, his account of another meeting steers things in a different direction.

Such evenings are made even more interesting by the odd slide show and the informal selling of bits and bobs. Someone might have a picture or two on display, while someone else may have brought hawking equipment along. I have to say, I am rarely tempted by such things, but at one meeting I found myself powerless to resist one of the splendid hand-made hunting knives on offer. But the pleasure of ownership was short lived. I had forgotten an important birthday, and, on getting back from the meet, I had to use the knife as a stand-in for the present I had neglected to buy.

Following an evening of celebration, the first hunting day will be an exciting affair and can begin in a number of ways. The falconer might find himself waking to the sound of calling hunting birds, these stimulated by the presence of their early-rising owners. I can even recall an occasion where we were woken by the mellow tones of a hunting horn drifting in through half-opened windows. Following the trail of notes, some of us eventually tracked down our mysterious musician. Deep in the parkland that housed the meeting, we discovered Josef Hiebeler standing under a gigantic tree. In the early morning light, all were captivated by this simple and moving scene. It was to be a performance repeated on a number of occasions, but never with the impact of that first time.

Hunting horns play a vital role in European falconry gatherings. They are used to open meetings, close them and are always blown over slain quarry. Dead quarry is, quite rightfully, treated with the greatest respect. It is not thrown into heaps or left in corners. At the end of each day, it is carefully laid out and acknowledged by those that have been involved in the killing of it. It is important to note that, at large meetings, the quarry remains the responsibility of officials, until the end of the meeting. Then it can be claimed by those who caught it. Leg tags are used to identify individual hares.

If the falconer finds himself at an international meeting, then the opening ceremony can be a pretty grand affair. Falconers and their birds are lined up in an orderly fashion, while opposite them, at some distance, visitors and local spectators observe the proceedings. Meeting officials will welcome all involved and open the gathering. Horns create a unique ambiance and several short speeches may be delivered before the hunt commences. At Opocno, the most important fixture in the European falconry calendar, this assembly takes place in the Schloss courtyard and what a dramatic and noble setting this makes. Some might find this type of ceremony over the top and unnecessary. But to those who take part, these established procedures are no chore. To participate is actually something of a honor.

With the formalities over, it is off to the hunting grounds. Each group will have an appointed leader and the identity of this person and his vehicle is worth discovering before "the off." Unless being taken to the hunting areas by specifically provided buses, falconers will be led, convoy fashion, in their own vehicles. Just how long the party remains in the field can vary from day to day and meet to meet. That said, days are normally long and it is not a bad idea to pack a bite to eat and perhaps something to drink in one's rucksack. A sandwich and a can of something will be additional ballast well worth carrying on a long day. Sometimes, it might be possible to circle round to the parked vehicles and take a lunchtime break there, but often any pauses or stops made will be in the field.

Back at base, one's presence will normally be required for the assembly that officially brings the day to a close and acknowledges the slain quarry. The day's bag will have been laid out and paid tribute to in the field (as always, with hunting horns), but at large meetings it will be displayed once again back at headquarters. Here, it will be placed alongside quarry taken by other groups. Each day generally follows a similar routine. Falconers gather with their birds in the morning for the official line-up, leave for the hunting grounds and assemble again at the close of the day. On the final day, all the quarry taken over the three-day period will be reverently laid out and what a grand sight this can make when the hunting has been good.

A Day in the Field

Looking back over the many hawking meets I have attended, I am reminded of some fine sport but it has not always been the best days that have earned themselves a place in the hawking diary. Some sessions have been recorded due to their odd or unusual nature and flicking back through my day book to the winter of 1994, I come to just such an occasion. It was a strange get-together in many respects and everything seemed against me actually attending. A last minute car problem resulted in me using someone else's vehicle. But this tiny replacement was not well suited to the task and with the eagle box loaded there was barely room for anything else. This was unfortunate, for I had two companions along for the one-day meeting and there was a journey of one and a half hours ahead of us.

Leaving Hohenwerfen and the mountains behind, we headed for flat, arable ground. However, although armed with a set of instructions and a map, we managed to get lost. Then with our course replotted and me trying to make up lost time, we were stopped by the police for speeding. The officers listened sympathetically, but fined me nonetheless. They also informed me that we were further away from our destination than I had imagined and now there seemed no possible way to arrive on time. The obvious thing to do was to stop and phone ahead, but even this proved difficult, and when I finally found a phone box I was beaten to it by an elderly couple whose pockets were loaded down with change. After waiting fifteen minutes it was clear that I was going to be in for a long wait. There was nothing to do but jump back in the car.

On and on we went through the rural countryside and not one single phone box did we pass. Things were getting desperate, we were now a half-hour late and it seemed fairly certain that the other falconers we were intending to meet would leave for the hawking grounds without us. I had to find a phone. Reluctant as I was, a private home seemed the only answer and it was now that we were to have a little bit of luck. Not only was the house owner willing to let me use the phone, he also knew where we were headed. We were in fact not ten minutes away. As it turned out the hawking party was just about to leave and the call saved the day.

Meeting at a restaurant on the out-skirts of a small town, we were quickly introduced to the rest of the party. Several falconers had brought falcons along and these were to hawk separately as a mini-group. The rest of us, flying four golden eagles, one red-tailed hawk and a goshawk, were placed together for hares. I was accompanied on this occasion by my girlfriend and an apprentice display falconer who was attending her first falconry meeting. She had never seen a hunting bird take quarry and so I hoped for a rewarding day. Astur was certainly keen, the weather was fine and, although the mixed group did not ideally suit me, I anticipated a good day in the field.

The hunting area was within walking distance so off we set. Due to our close proximity to the restaurant and neighboring houses, I imagined we would be in for quite a walk. But we were barely behind the restaurant before the hunt was declared open. A line was formed and we began to walk a rough grass field dotted with fruit trees. I could not believe it, we were almost in people's back gardens! Did the local hunter who was guiding the group really expect us to fly golden eagles here? Apparently he did for as a hare got up from almost under my feet he glanced at me in expectation—I glanced back in bewilderment. There was simply no way I was going to release Astur here. As we proceeded several more hares were flushed and some of the other eagle owners seemed happy to make an attempt at them, but Astur's hood remained in place.

As we moved on I had serious doubts about the day ahead. But fortunately our route soon brought us to a more appropriate area. Now I felt a little more relaxed and the red-tail owner on my right was also obviously happier about conditions for his hawk was soon in pursuit of its first hare. The bird was determined but no match for the animal she had set her sights on. She managed to get a foot to it but this strong winter hare shrugged her off with little effort. I wanted the red-tail to have success but the odds seemed stacked against her. She had spent four years in an aviary, had never previously taken quarry and was also quite small. As well as wishing the bird success, I hoped she would come through the day unscathed. She was in formidable company and one or two of the eagle owners were showing themselves to be less than professional. Two eagles had already come together and things were a little too relaxed for my liking.

The day in general was proving very frustrating. There were plenty of hares but the landscape was not at all well suited to eagle falconry. There were areas of good ground but one was never very far from some hazard; if not houses, then power lines. Some sections were crisscrossed with these deadly cables. It was a stop, start day and quite late into the hunt not a single hare had been taken. Condi-

140

tions had my apprentice disappointed and I could tell she was beginning to wonder if she would see anything caught. Her early enthusiasm on the wane, she needed to see something happen and she shortly did.

Again we entered a suitable area of country and again I geared myself for a flight. Ahead of us was a strip of woodland and it was toward this we were walking when a hare got up to my left. I was the first falconer in the line with just one beater beyond me. There was no question who this hare belonged to as it swung off back over the ground we had just walked. I unhooded the eagle. The plough was not particularly rough and the hare not particularly hindered, but as Astur bore down on it the quarry seemed unwilling to take evasive action. The distance between them shrank and Astur stormed in to master his victim.

After the catching of this first hare of the day followed a period of interesting flying which resulted in two hares being caught by other members of the group. But again the enjoyment was short-lived, up ahead of us were more dwellings. Surveying the scene, one could see what had happened. It was the familiar story of a village that had grown into a town, slowly swallowing up the countryside around it. The new houses we were approaching had been constructed on what must once have been quite suitable hare hawking ground. Miraculously the hares had remained but pursuing them with an eagle had been made almost impossible. I fully expected the group to be steered off in a safer direction but our guide wanted us to to work this section and was quite insistent. To my left was a road which led into the village and as we proceeded a hare flushed ahead of me. Boxed in by the falconers on my right, it took to the road and disappeared into the very town itself! Another peculiar incident quickly followed. Wheeling around to the right the group proceeded in a line which placed us adjacent to rear gardens. Up got another hare and after it, surprisingly, went an eagle. The eagle was unsuccessful but the hare was forced to make its escape across someone's lawn!

None of this worried me unduly, I simply was not flying. It was a difficult day and each falconer was going to have to make his own decisions about safety. My mind was clear, only the areas of open ground away from the town were of interest to me and it was on such an area that I had my next successful flight. I was standing almost alone as it had been decided to try to cover an enormous and promising-looking field in one sweep (a bit wasteful really). My hare, flushed by a lone beater, was some distance away. Like the first hare this one was running across plough but it was a field of deep, treacherous furrows. Ground conditions balanced out the long slip and although the hare made a valiant effort to avoid its pursuer, the experienced eagle was simply too much for her.

With Astur's second hare tucked away in the rucksack, we pushed on across the field. On the other side a jeep was waiting to relieve us of our quarry. Also waiting was a group of women who had been observing from the roadside. Not content to wait for our approach, one lady, complete with fur coat and best shoes, came across the field to meet us. Our spectators were fascinated by what we were doing and as they gathered around the air was soon filled with lively chatter. From a stream of jokes and humorous comments came offers of assistance—did we not need one or two more beaters?

Freeing ourselves from the talkative band we moved on. It was at this point that I elected to ease off and try to provide a suitable flight for one or two of the less successful birds. After all, I was a first-time guest and had already caught two hares. The first falconer I attempted to help was the goshawk owner. He had not had a single flight and so when a squatting hare was found quite near to me, I waved him over. He seemed a friendly chap and said that if his bird failed I should make an attempt with mine. I thanked him for the offer but suggested it would be too risky. Here, of course, I had calculated that the hawk would actually leave its owner's glove. It was a short slip, a prime chance and as the hare flushed I expected a burst of speed from the bird. Surely this king of short-winged hawks, with its dazzling acceleration and murderous lust to hunt, would make the most of the opportunity. With disbelieving eyes, I watched as the goshawk calmly observed her prey make its escape. She did not move a muscle!

Another bird that was experiencing a few problems was an immature female eagle, and when I found myself next to her owner I again tried to show a little consideration. With both of us flying out of the hood, I told him to fly at any hares that were mine or his, thereby doubling his chances. He was actually hunting with an assistant and, as the eagle was handed over to his helper, I presumed that this person would continue hunting with the bird. What a surprise then when a hare got up quite close to us and the fellow with the eagle did nothing. Instead the eagle's real owner rushed over and made a snatch for the bird's hood. Quite frankly I was speechless and amidst the confusion one very unconcerned hare made its way to safety.

A little bemused I decided to attempt the next hare myself. A chance soon came. Rising from the smooth earth ahead of me, a hare was hurrying away. His enthusiasm riding high from the last kill, Astur was off the glove almost before the hood was clear of his head. But enthusiasm and experience were not to prove sufficient. Skillfully calculating the eagle's approach, the hare prepared herself for the attack, her life depending on split-second timing. A move made too early would be followed by the eagle and a move made too late would be her undoing. Without altering course or speed, she waited for the bird to totally commit itself. Then with the eagle's giant, yellow feet almost on her, she made her move. Catapulting vertically, she jumped clean over her pursuer. She landed behind the eagle, paused for just a moment and then took off at speed.

For most of the day we had needed to fly extremely carefully to avoid dangerous power line situations. However, on taking a round-about route back to base we found ourselves being guided through an area where hunting should simply not have been attempted. Everywhere one looked there was high voltage wires. It was terribly annoying because hares were being flushed at regular intervals. Indeed, so tempting were these hares that one or two members of the group could not resist the urge to let their birds go. The area was scattered with trees and it was the presence of trees that made some of the falconers less worried about flying. They reasoned that following an unsuccessful flight their birds would be more likely to take perch in a tree than head for a mast. The trees around us certainly reduced the risk but they did not remove it and as far as I was concerned no hare was worth a dead eagle.

As we neared the vehicles I reflected on what a very strange day it had been. We had avoided houses, roads and power lines, and had come through it all without incident. More amazing, the group actually managed to take six hares. I had never hunted with an eagle in this fashion before, but if nothing else, it reminded me of my own good fortune. I have enjoyed the very best hare hawking in Europe; and such experiences do not belong in the past. Modern Europe may be changing, but the Continent still boasts ideal golden eagle landscapes and there are plenty of areas where even the largest eagle groups can find the freedom they require.

8   Rabbit Hawking

Generally speaking, I do not consider the European rabbit to be a truly suitable golden eagle quarry. Living in underground warrens and being reluctant to venture too far (by day) from some form of sanctuary makes it a less than ideal proposition for the eagle owner. For goshawks and Harris' hawks, the rabbit is a first class quarry, and, when pursued in enclosed country, perhaps even through tangled woods, the humble rabbit will provide excellent sport for these birds.

Nevertheless, rabbits can be hunted with eagles. In fact, in some settings, they are quite vulnerable to attacks from trained birds and can be taken in very much the same way as they are by wild-living eagles. In open hill country, rabbits can be found lying out in sparse cover well away from their warrens and it is when pursuing these rabbits that the eagle falconer can see some fine action (as can the buteo owner). This is not an aspect of eagle falconry I have practiced with any seriousness. Someone who has fully explored rabbit hawking with a golden eagle in hill country is Ron Moore of Great Britain; and it is to an article of his that appeared in the *Austringer* (the journal of the Welsh Hawking Club) that I now turn. Mr. Moore writes:

"Like most other falconers whenever I fly my birds I am more interested in seeing good flights and good flying style than coming home with a heavy bag. Once in a while, when quarry is fairly plentiful and weather conditions are perfect, the scene is set for a red-letter day. The following story is an account of such a day.

"It was at the beginning of March. The wind was very strong and in a south-westerly direction, just about perfect for flying the eagle on my best patch of flying ground which is very high up in the Yorkshire Dales.

"I rang up Steve Rhodes and asked him if he fancied a day out with the eagle. Steve was very keen to come, especially with the wind being so strong and in its present direction, so we loaded up the van and I went into the garden to weigh the eagle—she weighed just 4500 grams. When I put her back on her block she stood bolt upright, her lovely brown eyes were sparkling with excitement and her golden cape was slightly raised at the back of her head. She had just preened and oiled herself and was looking really magnificent. She had felt the wind in her face and had seen me collecting my gear so she knew that we were going hunting and was getting more excited by the minute. Strong winds always bring her into hunting condition, it is as if she knows that when strong winds blow she is in complete control of the skies, so rather than delay any longer I loaded her up and off we went.

"After a twenty mile (thirty-three kilometers) drive we arrived at our destination high in the Yorkshire Dales. We exchanged a word or two with the farmer and then set off to walk to the bottom of the high limestone crags. I always carry the eagle hooded until I get to the bottom of the crags as there are usually a few rabbits near the farm and I don't want her chasing them there for obvious reasons.

"On this particular day the wind was so strong that I could not keep her on my fist, so as soon as we were away from the farm I removed the swivel and leash and unhooded the eagle. She just looked around, opened her huge wings and lifted off my fist. She circled us once and then went right across the valley and disappeared from view over the cliffs.

"About two minutes later we saw her approximately 800 meters away heading into the wind, coming back towards us going higher and higher. At ground level the wind was so strong that Steve and I could hardly stand, so what it must have been like way above us I dreaded to think. I stood there for a few moments spellbound, watching the eagle effortlessly riding the currents and updrafts. Even after five years of flying her I still have nothing but admiration for her when she flies in a strong wind. Suddenly I was awakened from my day-dream by Steve shouting "Hare!" I looked around and spotted a rabbit running up the hillside. Looking up at the eagle I saw that by now she was in a vertical stoop, head-first, wings tightly tucked into her body. Just as she was about to level out and take the rabbit it shot into a wall. The eagle threw up and hung there in the wind. Suddenly she stooped again, this time there was no throw up so she must have taken it and as I climbed over the wall I spotted her ten meters away with her rabbit.

"When she had calmed down I removed the rabbit and gave her a reward. After she had eaten this I picked her up, cleaned her beak and held my hand up, her wings opened and away she went. I looked at my watch, we had been out for about five minutes and we'd had two good stoops.

"As I watched her mount up again, from nowhere a peregrine tiercel appeared. He must have been hunting nearby, spotted the eagle and decided to investigate. While I stood watching both of them Steve had disturbed another rabbit. Suddenly the eagle stooped, down she came with the peregrine in hot pursuit. For the first sixty meters or so the eagle left him standing, but as they neared the ground the eagle leveled out behind the rabbit and took it not ten meters from Steve's feet. The peregrine whistled past her and threw up right above her, beating into the wind and looking down at this strange bird in his hunting territory. After a couple of minutes he obviously decided that he had better get back to work, for the wife would not be too pleased if he was late back with the dinner!

"Again I let the eagle calm down and removed the rabbit, giving her a reward. I lifted her off the ground, cleaned her beak and held her up into the wind. Within ten seconds she had lifted off, again heading into the wind, going higher and higher. The day was living up to its promise and we were enjoying every minute of it.

"The wind was getting stronger, but the eagle was holding almost stationary above us, her great wings held right back along her body and her head moving from side to side scanning the ground below waiting for a rabbit to move. When she is up there you have to almost tread on a rabbit or hare before they will do so. I was admiring the way she controlled herself in the howling gale when suddenly she rolled over on to her back and came down head-first, twisting and turning. About twenty meters to my right I saw a rabbit going flat out heading for a pile of rocks. Looking at the distance that the eagle had to cover you would have thought that the rabbit would have made the safety of the rocks easily, but the speed of the eagle is so deceiving. The rabbit was only about half-way there when she took it with a tremendous smack. How such a big bird can maneuver in that way I just do not know, one second she was about one meter from the ground, still headlong and the next she was somersaulting with the rabbit. Again I let her calm down and removed the rabbit from her and after she had eaten her reward, which by the way is the skinned front leg of a rabbit, I picked her up and cleaned her beak. This time she just rubbed her beak on the back of my hand, looked around and lifted off.

"As Steve and I were discussing the last kill, we noticed the eagle again mounting up very quickly, boring into the wind and then climbing vertically on the sudden updrafts. She really was a sight to see. Sometimes, as she changed air currents, she would tuck her wings back into her body and shoot horizontally across the sky, only to turn and then come back right over us, waiting to be served.

"By now we were working on the side of a very steep rock scree. All at once the eagle stooped, there must have been a rabbit right at the top of the crags, she disappeared and then threw up again. Right above me I saw a rabbit leap into the air, it was obviously the quarry that had beaten the eagle the first time. The eagle closed up and stooped again, she appeared to miss the rabbit, but as she passed it, still head-first, I saw a big yellow foot shoot out and take the rabbit while it was still in mid-air. The eagle landed on the scree about fifteen meters below us, the wind was so strong that the only thing keeping her on the ground was the rabbit. I told Steve to sit down near me and we would wait for the eagle to take her kill to a calmer spot. As we sat there the eagle looked up at us and started to come up the hill towards us dragging the dead rabbit. When she got right to my feet she laid the rabbit down across my boots and started to plume it. I moved back a little, took a fresh front leg off a rabbit, then I removed the kill and rewarded the eagle.

"By now I was beginning to wonder how long the eagle would hunt. After all, she had four front legs of rabbit in her crop and at four and a half kilograms was in fairly high hunting condition. However, she was eager to keep going, so up she went and we set off beating for her—this time heading back towards the farm which was nestling down in the valley far below us.

"Suddenly a rabbit broke cover below us, down came the eagle at a forty-five degree angle, this time feet first. She passed across us at tremendous speed, the noise of the wind passing through her primaries was quite frightening. As the eagle was about to commit herself and go in to foot, the rabbit dived under a pile of rocks and was safe. The eagle just turned out over the valley, gained height and came back over us again.

"We hadn't gone more than fifty meters when the eagle shot down-wind, stopped dead and stooped vertically down into the rocks far below. When we arrived on the scene she was holding her fifth rabbit in one foot. I told Steve that I would take the rabbit from her and watch her reactions. If I thought that she still wanted to hunt then I would let her. After removing the rabbit and rewarding her I felt her crop. It was about half full, but she still wanted to go so I thought I would risk it.

"Up she went again, this time my eyes never left her, I was watching for the tell-tale signs that meant she was losing her edge. Within half a minute we were treated to the most spectacular sight that I have ever seen in falconry. She was just coming over us at a very high pitch, her head was forward and her wings were tucked tightly into her body, when suddenly she dropped one wing and fell sideways out of the sky. Down she came at tremendous speed, twisting and turning keeping herself perfectly balanced in the howling gale. Just when I thought she was about to smash herself into the rocks above us she rolled over on one side, leveled out and plucked a fleeing rabbit from the very edge of a sheer drop. She swung round with the rabbit in her talons and landed right under the very tops of the high limestone cliffs. It was the most breathtaking thing that either of us had ever seen, an almost unbeatable feat of flying and a fitting end to a most memorable day.

"I climbed up to her, removed the rabbit with her usual reward and then cut the warm rabbit up and fed her up. As she was feeding I glanced at my watch and got the shock of my life. We had been flying for just one hour and in that time she had taken six rabbits in truly classic style. We had been flying in some of the most remote and beautiful countryside that you could ever wish to see and had seen, to my mind, one of nature's most spectacular fliers performing in her element."

9 Cast Flights

Whether it is feasible or not to fly two golden eagles together as a cast is a topic not infrequently discussed. My own experience of true cast flights is limited to just one single attempt. This attempt took place in Bavaria, Germany, and, at the time, I was working at a commercial falcony center, Schloss Rosenburg. This was an establishment where the practical side of falconry was very important and a good deal of hawking was done with hand-reared golden eagles.

In 1986, the center's proprietor, Josef Hiebeler and I were faced with rearing and training two newly "recruited" male eagles. We named these birds Khan and Tzari (Khan belonging to me), and, rather than work with them individually, we decided to try to bring them along together. Initially, we had our sights set on little more than joint training flights. But as things progressed, flights to quarry began to seem quite feasible.

The eagles spent their early days in the castle's busy inner courtyard. This, separate from the main flying area, had been the setting for the rearing of countless eagles, vultures and other raptors. The courtyard was well designed for the purpose of rearing for, although young birds could be guaranteed safety and protection, they were not robbed of visual stimulation in the form of other birds, visitors, members of staff and working dogs. Later, they were housed alongside each other under a long, spacious lean-to, this divided in

151

half by a low barrier that did not prevent the eagles seeing one another. Of course, the length of each bird's leash was calculated so as to keep them well apart. When the time came for flight training, Hiebeler and I initially worked with our birds individually. Only once each bird had gained a little flying skill and was coming well to the fist and lure did we begin flying both eagles together.

With lure-work, our main worry was that one bird might injure the other, and, with this in mind, we approached training very carefully indeed. To begin with, we simply got both eagles to feed from separate areas of the same lure-carcass. In an effort to keep things totally under control, the eagles' movements were restricted by holding their jesses short (each of us securing one bird). Things went remarkably well and we were soon enjoying some fine motorized lure flights. The procedure was very much the same as working with one bird, except here two were released simultaneously. With them spaced several meters apart, the eagles were unhooded to take on a joint direct flight to a single lure. Neither bird ever attempted to get at the other, but, playing safe, a hawking bag was always slipped between them as they sat on the lure. So that this could be done quickly, one of us always acted as lure-man, leaving an assistant to fly his bird. To pull the lures (roe and fox), we used a range rover, and, with the tail-gate in its down position, the rear of the vehicle made a fairly stable platform for the sitting lure-man. This position also made judging the speed of flights a little easier. However, I do remember that, at one end of the field, there was a slight hummock, and, as the birds gained fitness and the flights became longer, the bump frequently resulted in a rather uncomfortable finish to a flight!

Lure-work was, of course, just one aspect of training. Joint soaring sessions were also undertaken with both birds being allowed to soar from the castle (this situated on the side of a valley) for what became quite extended periods. During these sessions, both of us would be on hand to intervene should anything go wrong. Initially, both birds were quite reluctant to take full advantage of the liberty being allowed them. Once released from the castle, one or both of them might complete a short flight before returning to where they had flown from. Then might follow a rest period either on the fist or the castle wall. Generally, if one bird flew, so did the other. Indeed, the sight of one bird soaring always motivated the other to get airborne, and, in this respect, the eagles often kept each other on the wing.

Early fights did not see the birds particularly high above the Schloss itself, but this was of no importance. Rosenburg's lofty position guaranteed that as soon as they left its valley-facing walls, they immediately had considerable height. The terrain simply dropped away below them. True high altitude flights came later as the young aviators gained experience and became more adventurous.

With the training of these birds, we were fortunate in many ways. For example, everything required was close to hand. We could soar (weather permitting) straight from the Schloss, could conduct motorized lure-work on an area of ground within walking distance and we also had plenty of mixed and broad-leaved woodland to fly in. But of equal importance was the fact that Hiebeler and I could train together every day. Naturally, we both had other commitments at the castle, but setting aside time for training was not difficult. As we geared up for hunting, training became quite intense, the friendly competition that developed between us intensifying things still further.

This competition saw both of us indulging in private, individual training sessions. We followed the same guidelines, but each believed he had his own secret formula for putting on the finishing touches. My routine was quite straightforward—I kept the bird active and in the air as much as possible! Although I was extremely enthusiastic about joint training periods, I must confess that solitary outings brought their own rewards. When sneaking off for a spot of private flying, my procedure was always the same. Outside the castle gates, the drive sloped gradually down towards the field where lure training was conducted. In places, this drive was covered by a high canopy of trees, these forming a huge, natural tunnel. Down the drive I would march, releasing Khan about three quarters of the way down. Familiar with the routine, he always powered away under the canopy to break out into the open space of the terrain beyond. The land itself dipped slightly, and, flying hard, he would use this to gain some height. With the eagle still going away from me, I would emerge from the trees and wait for what I knew would follow. Banking over, he began his long approach back to the fist. His return was never a leisurely affair: aided by height, his accelerating approach would eat up the distance between us.

These private training sessions included all of the normal elements, such as following on along the woodland edge and a few fist flights. But eventually, I nearly always found myself in a quiet, reflective mood, looking back at the castle from a small, grassy hill. With the eagle on my arm, I would survey the scene and it was a scene not without interest. The castle, with its creamy-colored walls, stood out boldly against the surrounding woodland and the picture was often complemented by a trained vulture soaring high above the valley.

Heading back, the eagle would again be given some freedom, but a little caution had to be exercised. Sometimes, my return to the castle coincided with someone leaving in the range rover. Repeated lure flights using this vehicle had geared the bird to respond immediately. On a couple of occasions, he peeled off to double check it was towing nothing behind it. With his curiosity satisfied, he then returned.

Back at the castle, the peace of my solitary sessions would be shattered by the rush of activity. Of the three falconry centers I have been involved with, Rosenburg in Bavaria was by far the busiest. The displays really were incredible and carefully calculated to give maximum effect. They involved large numbers of birds and a full team of staff. Summertime displays put one under a lot of pressure. Hiebeler was always aiming for perfection and a below-standard performance would result in members of staff being given a good dressing down. But he rarely had need to complain and the place was always swamped with visitors.

As well known as Rosenburg was for display work, it was even better known in the hawking community as a center for top class eagle falconry. During the hunting season, as many as five golden eagles might be based at the castle and it was not unusual for three or four Rosenburg eagles to be taken to a falconry meeting.

The training of Tzari and Khan coincided with a special time at the Schloss and I suppose things had slowly reached some kind of pitch. Much had certainly been accomplished. Hunting eagles from the castle had been doing remarkably well in various parts of Europe. Indeed, it seemed that Rosenburg eagles could do no wrong. On the display side, great things had also been achieved. It was a period that saw the acquisition of a young lammergeier, or bearded vulture, which was reared and trained with enormous success. I believe only one other was then being flown in Europe for demonstration work and this made the experience even more precious. Much of the lammergeier's basic training was conducted by myself and colleague Martin Müller. Both of us found the work extremely rewarding and to finally see our pupil out in the valley soaring with the center's other vultures (European black and griffon) brought a great sense of satisfaction.

For the 1986 hunting season, eagles had been shuffled slightly. A mature female that Hiebeler had been working with was set aside for breeding purposes. It was a shame to loose this bird from the team, for she rarely disappointed, and, with her, Hiebeler had enjoyed a terrific season in 1985. When flown from the fist to brown hares, this medium-sized female was really potent; at one meeting, she actually had people shaking their heads in disbelief.

The team now included, in addition to the two youngsters, two experienced males. One of these was not technically a Rosenburg eagle. He actually belonged to Jürgen Färber, but, more often than not, was housed at Rosenburg. During the summer in particular, Färber preferred to keep the bird where he could see plenty of activity. Färber's routine would then be to come up to the castle and prepare for hunting using Rosenburg as a base. His eagle was extremely good. Trained at the castle as a youngster, his inborn talent was soon recognized and he was, of course, given every chance to develop it. To my mind, this eagle was perfectly built: rakish and sharp looking, with huge feet. The other male belonged to castle worker Lisa Gasslbauer. He was flown primarily to hares, but had also taken a number of foxes and was certainly not short on courage. This eagle was remarkably easy to manage, but, although he would fly for any member of staff, it seemed that he only pulled out all the stops when being handled by Gasslbauer.

As important as the two experienced males were, in 1986, Khan and Tzari took priority, and, after a lot of hard work, it was soon time to put theory into practice by testing them against wild quarry. Although we had trained primarily with fox and roe deer lures, we actually had brown hares in mind and so it was hare flights we sought. Now the potential we had witnessed during lure flights fully expressed itself and how impressive they were to watch as they closed with fast, open country hares. As with lures, there was no fighting on quarry; nevertheless, on arriving at the scene of a kill, one of us would slip a hawking bag between them just as we had done during training. Actually removing them from a kill was a relatively simple task. One of us would remove one bird first and move away from the scene. His colleague would then take up the other eagle and put the hare in his hawking bag.

We took our eagles to two falconry meetings. This was accomplished in one extended trip, and, with Gasslbauer and her more experienced eagle along, Hiebeler and I were not under quite so much pressure with the youngsters.

The first meeting was in Austria, and, as this was the first time the youngsters would be scrutinized by outside falconers, Hiebeler and I were both enthusiastic and perhaps a little apprehensive. How would they perform? We began to prepare for the trip, and, as familiar checklists were gone through, an atmosphere of excitement started to build. Hunting trips from Rosenburg always felt a little like expeditions, and, when traveling far from home, one could not afford to forget anything. The expedition vehicle would be a green minibus, and, if carefully loaded, this would carry five people, four eagles and all the equipment and clothing required. The eagles traveled in transport boxes and these were loaded in a block of four at the rear of the bus.

The day before a journey would find the bus parked in the inner courtyard, being cleaned out and checked over. The transport boxes were stored above a workshop, and, with the bus ready, these would be loaded. When one thinks of a hunting bus, one can easily visualize

156

a battered vehicle, stuffed full of muddy boots and goodness knows what else. But this was not the way things were done at Hiebeler's center. When prepared for a hawking trip, the Rosenburg bus sparkled inside and out. The packing of equipment followed a carefully laid out plan. There was a place for everything and everything had its place. The eagles' perches were always a bit awkward to wedge into their slots. These were matching ring perches, finished in dark green and each carrying the Rosenburg emblem in its center. At meetings, these perches would be positioned, whenever possible, in a straight line. Spaced with the utmost precision, they made an impressive sight when occupied by three or four eagles. This may sound all a little ostentatious, but Hiebeler was proud of Rosenburg and had good reason to be. However, by parading in this fashion, Rosenburg had to make sure that the flamboyant flair exhibited at the weathering area was backed up in the field by good practical hawking. The mini-bus also carried the Rosenburg emblem, as did the hunting waistcoats of employees.

For this particular trip, two vehicles were being used. Hiebeler and I were traveling in the bus with the three eagles, while Gasslbauer, who had planned to call in at a friend's home, drove her own transport.

The Austrian meeting was a three-day affair and was based at a renovated *schloss*. This was a beautiful building and decorated inside as it was with various flags and tapestries, it made a very appropriate headquarters for the gathering. However, it did have one major disadvantage: it was surrounded by a broad, water-filled moat and this made the constructing of a weathering lawn almost impossible. Several falconers had managed to squeeze their birds in along the narrow strip of ground that immediately encircled the *schloss*. One person had even found enough space for an eagle. But for the majority of birds, there was simply no room. Fortunately, one of the participating falconers owned a riding school, and, as this was nearby, it seemed the most logical answer. On arriving at this equestrian center, we were all most impressed. It was huge and had every conceivable facility. So with plenty of space and ample security, this became the official weathering area. Nevertheless, as suitable as the

157

riding school was, this confusion about where to house the birds demonstrated very poor planning indeed.

Arrangements had been made for the falconers themselves to stay in local hotels and this resulted in a rather hectic start to each day. One would hurriedly eat breakfast, drive to the riding school, collect one's bird and then drive on again to meet up with other falconers at the *schloss*. There was one more little annoyance. The hunting areas were located an unbelievably long way from base. However, out in the field, these little niggles were soon forgotten, for the hawking conditions on the first day were ideal. There was hardly any wind, the terrain was well-drained, open, arable land and hares were plentiful.

My colleagues and I found ourselves in a group containing five or six golden eagles. One of these, I recall, was a youngster being flown by Claus Fentzloff. This new eagle was replacing a bird he had been flying for over twenty years. Another far less welcome character was a chain-smoking Austrian. If there is one thing I find really aggravating, it is someone smoking during the hunt and this chap never seemed to have a cigarette out of his mouth. Also, he obviously took as much care of his bird as he did of his health: the poor thing was smashed to pieces. Its plumage was in a frightful state. Most annoying of all was that this falconer, blundering about the field, actually managed to account for quarry!

Hiebeler and I were flying our birds separately and the first hare we caught was taken in deep roots by my bird. This hare, sitting tight, got up behind me, but traveled only a short distance before being taken. Root crops were to provide us with a good many flights on that first day, and, at one point, the group was split up to work individual strips. Here, I found myself allocated an entire strip to myself, and, with an obliging falconer working his English pointer for me, I was given plenty of opportunities. Hares were breaking left and right heading for fast, smooth terrain, but each time the eagle just hit short of his mark. A couple of the other eagles were successful, including Gasslbauer's bird, which took one hare, a hare that unfortunately was to prove his last of the meeting. On his very next flight, he injured a wing. It was nothing too serious, but it put him temporarily out of action.

On day two, Hiebeler and I were in a smaller group; in fact, we were the only eagle owners in our party. Under these conditions, we decided to attempt a few joint flights, and, positioned at opposite ends of the hawking line, we readied ourselves for a hare. The landscape was spacious, unrestricted and vegetation of any kind was thin on the ground. The first hare to get up was flown at, but missed by both birds. The second flight had a different outcome. It was a long slip made feasible by our slightly elevated location. The hare's position favored Khan and he made contact first. He hit the hare hard, and, on the parched earth, a shower of soil fragments was sent flying into the air. But he had taken the hare badly, leaving Hiebeler's bird, powering in seconds later, to secure a head hold.

This first successful flight met with a good deal of enthusiasm from the rest of our party. This was all very new to them and they were loving every minute of it. Even when a hare was missed, the joint attacks were of great interest, as were the return flights. Our spectators found it amusing that, following a defeat, the eagles sometimes ended up with the "wrong" owners. They responded equally well to both of us, and, after a long flight, it was not easy to pick out which bird was which. It was not until the wrong bird was coming into the glove that the mistake was realized. A quick change over and the hunt could continue.

This type of confusion resulted in an amusing moment. A hare was missed and I found myself having to deal with two returning eagles. My own bird had landed back on the glove as normal, when I noticed Tzari coming toward me. With Khan having consumed his tidbit, I simply put up my other arm and let Tzari land on it. Although protected with just a jacket sleeve, I had no worries about this mild-mannered bird.

But we were there to fly hares, not amuse the crowd and during the afternoon, we had some fine coursing-type flights. Most were fairly long and fast and ground conditions suited the quarry perfectly. One flight was to a hare moving swiftly over the smooth terrain. Separated by the line of beaters-*cum*-spectators, Hiebeler and I re-

159

acted almost simultaneously and both birds were away. The hare was running as straight as an arrow. With no cover ahead of it, the only way it was going to save itself was to either out-distance or out-maneuver its pursuers. Had the quarry been situated centrally between the two eagles, their individual routes would have seen them converging as they neared the target. But this was not the case. The hare got up nearer to Hiebeler, presenting his bird with an almost direct flight and requiring mine to cut slightly across the field. As Tzari bore down on the hare, it veered off to the right, and, as it did so, Khan charged straight into it. It was practically a collision, with the poor hare absorbing the impact. But Tzari was not going to be denied: having stayed airborne, he too came thundering in.

Flying our birds together, we enjoyed a few successful flights during the course of the meeting and were extremely pleased with their rather public performance. But our hawking was not concluded with the finish of this Austrian meet. We had another meeting to attend in Czechoslovakia (Slovakia), and, as this was not due to begin for a few days, we decided to take a break at Petronell, this being a short distance from the Czechoslovakian border. During this time, Gasslbauer drove back in her own vehicle to Bavaria, leaving her injured bird with Hiebeler and I. Having made no hunting arrangements for this short interlude, we had to content ourselves with a few training flights, but after the active few days we had experienced, this was no major inconvenience. Indeed, as it turned out, some of the training sessions were extremely interesting in their own right. We located a small hill, and, when the wind picked up one afternoon, we made for this higher ground to give our eagles an opportunity to soar. The birds were allowed individual sessions, and, for these, we had an unexpected guest. Where he came from I have no idea, but suddenly up there on that wind-swept hill was a small, rather frail-looking old man. He was absolutely mesmerized by the sight of a high-flying eagle savoring the heavy winds that now prevailed. We later discovered that our guest had initially believed the eagle he was watching to be a wild bird. This then explained his reaction when a lure was tossed out and the eagle came in dramatically from above. I thought he was going to pass out!

160

Our brief stay in Petronell had been pleasant, but it was soon time to move on. Ernst Lüttger was expecting us on the other side of the border in Bratislava. Interestingly enough, after meeting up with him, we managed to cram in a spot of impromptu hare hawking. Lüttger himself had to remain in Bratislava, but he told us where we might obtain a flight or two, and, following his advice, Hiebeler and I eventually found ourselves trying to locate hares along the river Danube. This was all a little peculiar, made more so by the failing light and the handful of local children we had roped in as beaters. The area was dry and littered with scrubby vegetation and its width allowed us plenty of room to operate. We split up and commenced the hunt. I say "hunt," but what we were engaged in was about as far removed from serious hawking as anything could be. There was no real order or planning: both of us were simply desperate to try to catch something, and, with darkness approaching, the pace became frantic. Our enthusiastic beaters were half to blame: as they crashed and rummaged through the scrub, we could hardly keep up with them!

Unfortunately, hares were scarce. We only found two and, as the first one was flushed, youthful screams of delight accompanied it on its way. It was also accompanied by the two eagles. The scene was one of utter chaos. From a distance, we must have looked like a bunch of lunatics. No one seemed to know exactly where the hare had gone. One moment it was there, the next lost in the scrub. However, both birds were already in full pursuit and their individual attack routes made an interesting picture in the dwindling light. Released from different locations, Khan's path took him round the scrub, Tzari's over it. The first attempt, coming from above, took the form of a sudden, sharp plunge as the hare raced through the high cover. But Tzari's attack was foiled and the hare, still invisible to us, was obviously still on the move. Now making a rushing assault was my bird, but again the hare proved too skillful and the cover too demanding.

By the time the second and final hare was come across (on our way back to the vehicle), it was almost too dark to see it, let alone fly at it. We had to admit defeat. As unsuccessful as the outing had been, taking part had obviously thrilled our troop of helpers to bits. But whether their account of the bizarre hunt was later believed by others, we will never know.

The meeting we had been invited to attend was due to start the following day and so, that evening, with Lüttger leading the way, we headed for where the get-together was being held. There, we met up again with Gasslbauer, and, with her bird now passed fit to fly, our team was complete. The meeting itself turned out to be an enjoyable one, but with a large number of eagles present, any sort of serious cast flying was deemed inadvisable. That said, all our eagles took quarry and the traveling break at Petronell and the mini-hunt along the Danube had made the whole expedition well worth while.

In trying to assess Khan and Tzari, one would have to say that they were not flown long enough together for any accurate conclusions to be drawn. Here, one must also bear in mind, they were two young eagles making all the mistakes that young eagles make. What might have developed or shown itself had they been allowed to gain experience together over a longer period of time is impossible to calculate. What one can say is that, generally, the slightly smaller eagle, flown by me, demonstrated a little more commitment when taking on direct pursuit-type flights. He was certainly the faster of the two birds. This slight speed advantage had not been obvious during motorized lure flights, but was quite noticeable when hunting. These eagles differed too in temperament: neither was difficult in any way, but the smaller bird was of a more active disposition. The two eagles eventually went to colleagues who flew them separately with continued success. Sadly, Hiebeler's male was killed by a female eagle in 1993.

Moving on from true cast flights, one occasionally hears of two eagles that are sometimes flown at quarry together, but have not been specifically trained for joint flights. Just recently, a British falconer was telling me of the success he had experienced flying a male and female eagle together. These birds were imported from a breeder in Germany, but when he acquired them, their new owner had no plans to attempt any kind of double eagle flights; and naturally, few people would automatically consider this type of thing as even a remote possibility. Nevertheless, these birds displayed such sympathetic behavior toward each other that joint training sessions were carefully planned. From these, I understand, developed a situation where the two birds could be flown without incident to hares. However, although the female eagle was apparently safe to fly with her own male, she attempted to kill another individual.

A couple of seasons ago, I was out with an eagle group that contained two adult males that their owners described as being safe in each other's company. On this particular day, the one eagle was known to be too high in weight, but not sufficiently so to warrant it being left at home. As we proceeded across open country, the overweight eagle found itself being carried along the edge of a deep, cover-filled ditch. To the left, the next eagle in line was the other male eagle that formed this rather loose two-bird partnership. My own position placed me further still to the left (carrying another male eagle).

Suddenly, there was movement in the ditch and this caused the falconer with eagle number one to release his bird, although no quarry was actually visible. His eagle left the fist, but went into a low, spindly tree growing from the side of the ditch. At the same moment as the bird landed in the tree, a roe deer emerged from the ditch heading right and going away from the hawking party. The tree-sitting eagle remained motionless, but thinking quickly, its owner shouted to his hesitant colleague to fly his bird and this he did. Although the deer was covering ground at a reasonable pace, it was obviously not fit and carrying some sort of injury and this was to be its undoing. Eagle number two made up the distance and brought the deer down. The first eagle now left its branch to join its companion on the kill, contenting itself with the rear of the quarry. What happened next was as interesting as the actual flight. Instead of both falconers hot-footing it to the scene, the owner of the bird that first took the deer remained rooted to the spot, leaving his colleague to reach and dispatch the quarry alone. So, not only did the falconer with the overweight eagle initiate the flight, he also brought it to a close. I later learned that the other falconer's slow response was due to the fact that he was recovering after damaging one of his legs in a fall. Although he could walk, he was apparently unable to run.

A rather unique experience was had by German falconer Gerhard Vogt. A breeder of golden eagles, he flew a mother and daughter together, both for training and hunting. No animosity was witnessed and the adult, who was more than fifteen years old, also became tolerant of other juvenile eagles; their distinctive plumage apparently acting as a signal. The Vogt birds were demonstrating a natural mother\daughter understanding. In the wild state young eagles are known to occasionally join adults in attacks on quarry. Some of these hunts involve the youngster playing a minor role, but in others, it can be fully involved. The two and three birds assaults on large mammals probably occur in this way. During this period of dependency, bonds are formed that may last a considerable time. Many young eagles separate from the adults quite early but family groups will sometimes spend the first winter together, and loose associations extending even further are known.

But care must be taken not to assume too much, especially from the falconer's point of view. It would, for example, be most unwise to draw comparisons between *chrysaetos* and the gregarious Harris' hawk. Although it may sometimes be possible to fly two golden eagles together, I personally feel (regardless of my own single successful attempt) that these birds are far better off hunted with individually. When two eagles are employed together, the slightest mistake or miscalculation can have disastrous consequences, as the following example will illustrate. A male and female eagle, which were frequently flown in each other's company, were taken out for a day's hawking. The idea was to put both birds into the trees, but as the first hawking spot visited seemed of limited interest, only one bird, the female, was allowed to fly. The male was kept (hooded) on the fist as the party continued, with the female eagle following on through the trees. At a small clearing, the party paused, the female above them. Ahead lay a small area of cover, the sort of cover the female eagle had learned to associate with quarry. Now with her anticipating a flight, two things happened to trigger an automatic response. Her owner moved suddenly toward his colleague who was carrying the male eagle and at the same moment, this bird, although hooded, bated. In a flash, the female left the tree and ploughed into the male. Miraculously, no permanent damage was done to either bird, but from that day on they were flown separately.

10 Taking up off Quarry

Physically removing quarry from an eagle is not a particularly difficult task for any determined falconer. Repeatedly taking an eagle off
quarry without causing resentment requires a little skill.

Training for this really starts with early lure work, with the
falconer taking his bird up off lures and carcasses. If this has been
done with care, then removing the eagle from its kills should run
smoothly. The principal is basically the same. The eagle is offered
substitute meat (held in the gloved hand) and, as it comes onto the
fist for this, its trainer moves over the quarry shielding it from the
bird. At this point, if the victim is a rabbit or hare, it can be wriggled
into the hawking bag. The secret here is to get the quarry into the bag
quickly, but without the bird seeing it. This is not too difficult if a
low squatting or kneeling position is held and one's body is employed as a shield. It is vitally important that the bird be totally
unaware of the deceitful business its trainer's free hand is occupied
with.

When hawking hares, I tend to use a standard shoulder-carried
hawking bag and a rucksack. At the scene of a kill, I remove the bag
and place the quarry in this to begin with. At some convenient
moment, I hood the eagle and transfer the hare to the rucksack. Even
the weight of one hare in a normal hawking bag can be a burden. On
one's back, the distributed weight is far more comfortable to carry.

With larger quarry, help is always welcome, not only from the carrying point of view, but also when taking the bird up. The assistant hides the kill, leaving the falconer to concentrate solely on his bird. If hawking large quarry alone, one can use the hood as an aid. The bird is taken up in the normal manner, but hooded before any attempt is made to do anything with the kill. Again, the falconer's body is used to prevent the eagle seeing the dead quarry and attempting to get back to it.

I think the less experienced falconer often confuses removing kills with actually robbing his bird. I suppose technically one is stealing the kill, but if it is done with feeling, it will have no adverse effects on the bird. If the eagle is educated correctly, the speed with which it will come off quarry is quite surprising. However, if removed incorrectly, resentment will certainly build and the relationship between man and bird will degenerate to a point where neither party finds the hawking experience a rewarding one. The eagle's manners will suffer (both at home and in the field) and it will become increasingly possessive of kills. Now, the taking up procedure will resemble a tug of war, rather than a smooth, professional operation.

Feeding up on Kills

The main argument for feeding up on kills is that the bird will be encouraged by the experience; and what could leave a more positive impression on a young eagle in sharp hunting condition than warm, bloody flesh? Basically, the principle is a sound one, but it does need to be operated with a little common sense. Allowing an eagle to eat repeatedly as much as it wishes from its first and only kill of the day achieves nothing except to rob the eagle and falconer of valuable field time. The hunting experience can be made worthwhile for the eagle without it always needing to gorge itself to a standstill.

A reliable procedure when working with relatively inexperienced eagles is to make a small incision in the quarry and allow the bird to feed here for a while before tempting it on to the fist with substitute meat. Once the eagle is achieving some degree of field success, this type of thing can stop. The quarry is simply dispatched and the bird taken up. However, this does not mean that, once the

167

eagle starts to become effective as a hunter, all feeding from quarry should cease. With large and demanding quarry, the eagle should always be fed something from its kill. In the case of the roe deer, I allow the eagle to feed from the opened up throat and under jaw area. With roe deer, the falconer should never miss an opportunity to strengthen his bird's commitment to this quarry. Pelts with heads attached should be used regularly during non-hunting periods and even individual roe heads (chopped lengthwise in half) can be used.

I am a great believer in reinforcing an eagle's drive to hunt and this applies no matter how experienced the bird may be. An eagle used for hunting large quarries does of course deserve special attention but even when a bird is being flown primarily as a hare hawk it should not be neglected. Its kills, if correctly dealt with, can be put to very good use. Brown hares, like roe deer, make fine fare for the table. But any hare destined for the kitchen should be skinned with care so as to remove the pelt almost in one piece and leaving, as always, the head attached . If done skillfully, the chest section of the pelt will finish up as a type of pouch and into this one can push additional loose meat. For example, the vital organs removed from the animal's chest cavity can now be put back into this part of the pelt. To keep them in place the pelt is tied in a large knot. When finished it may appear a very curious creature but to an eagle it will be irresistible.

The eagle is required to make just one flight to this type of hare lure. The bird is then secured and allowed to devour its meal. Before the flight I take a knife to the hare's head to help the bird gain access. The head is left entire but partially opened. The lure line is not fixed around the hare's neck but fed through a small hole made in the head wherever convenient. I prefer to use a length of heavy cord which is simply pulled loose once the bird is on the hare. I use my gloved hand to keep the lure still as I tear the cord free with my right hand. The cord is removed so that there is no risk of the bird becoming tangled up in it.

These flights are staged at home and so the falconer can have the lure caught where he wants. This means that the eagle's normal lawn perch can be repositioned and placed near the spot where the falconer plans the flight to end. A simulated struggle can have the bird moved a meter or two so that it can be secured with snap-clip swivels and a leash to its perch. This done (with lure cord removed) the eagle is left alone. Use of the gloved hand may be required to initiate feeding but basically the bird is left to its own devices. In possession of the hare, the eagle will be occupied for some time, and should not be disturbed until it finishes its meal. This meal will prove a satisfying one, for a hungry eagle will consume the whole thing. All that will remain will be scattered clumps of fur.

This sort of work should not be confused with true lure training. Lure training is there to orientate birds to fur and to develop fitness and flying skills. They are not single flights and the bird is not left alone with the lure; it is rewarded from the lure by the falconer and removed ready for another flight. When feeding upon a prepared hare pelt the falconer's objectives are quite different. The bird should be made to work for the lure but the main point is for the eagle to feel satisfied. One hard and well rewarded flight is required; a flight that will leave a lasting impression. It is a procedure that is especially valuable when an eagle has experienced a run of bad luck. But a hare pelt can also be used after an extended period of successful hawking which finishes, for some reason, with the bird not rewarded in the field. Then, a prepared hare pelt given at home will quickly balance things out.

Whenever the hawking schedule allows, feeding upon hare pelts will help keep a bird motivated. It takes little time to arrange such flights and the bird will benefit so very much from them. An eagle handled in this way will always display more drive than the bird that is constantly fed on the fist.

11 Other Eagles

Modern European and North American falconry sees many nontraditional hunting birds employed (and of course hybrids); and, in other parts of the world, one finds falconers using hawks and falcons that have no historical ties with hawking at all. This applies to eagles, too. Some of those who have seen golden eagles in action have naturally been quite keen to explore how effective other large, powerful species might be. Here, some of the big African and South American eagles come to mind, birds completely unknown to ancient falconers. Those desiring to take large, mammalian quarries, but living in areas where the traditional golden eagle does not naturally occur, have had to look to indigenous alternatives. These alternative eagles, being flown to quarries they are familiar with and functioning under geographical and climatic conditions that they are perfectly suited to, have shown themselves to be quite worthwhile propositions.

The large African Verreaux's eagle resembles the golden eagle in shape (and, of course, is closely related), but its black and white adult plumage gives it a more striking appearance. This bird has been used successfully in its native homeland. Some years ago, an Austrian colleague of mine flew a female to brown hares in central and eastern Europe. Hunting from the fist, this bird did quite well against hares and I even recall watching her take hold of a large fox. This

170

she sadly lost due to some fool late slipping a female golden eagle. The result was that the golden eagle grabbed the Verreaux's and the fox escaped. Luckily, neither bird sustained any serious injury.

The impressive hunting capabilities of birds like the forest-living African crowned eagle and the larger, open country African martial eagle have not gone unnoticed by modern falconers. But far more seriously used has been the much smaller African hawk-eagle. This swift eagle lacks nothing in terms of fire and hunting drive and has been used very successfully in its natural haunts. Surprisingly enough, it has even been flown at night. Night hunting involves the use of a spot-light, the bird being flown to hares illuminated in the beam. This eagle has also taken quarry under European falconry conditions. Bonelli's eagle, too, has been flown by European falconers. Whether Bonelli's and the African hawk-eagle are separate species or one and the same (the African hawk-eagle simply being a sub-species) is open to debate.

The wedge-tailed eagle of Australia, southern New Guinea and Tasmania is a sizable, well-armed bird. Its potential as a falconry bird has not been fully tested in Europe, but it is certainly an eagle worthy of consideration. Of far less interest are the imperial eagle of Europe and Asia and the tawny eagle of eastern Europe, central Asia, India and Africa. Tawny eagles from eastern Europe and central Asia are commonly referred to as steppe eagles, but are classed as the same species. The imperial and tawny eagle (steppe eagle) are of no real value from a falconry point of view and in attempting to hunt with them, the falconer is making life very difficult for himself. As a rabbit or hare hawk, one of the more spirited buteos or a female goshawk will prove far superior, giving a much better return for the time invested.

An eagle that has definite traditional ties with falconry is the mountain hawk-eagle. In Japan, this powerful hawk-eagle has long been employed to hunt hares. Even raccoon dogs and foxes have been accounted for with this bird. Although never as widely utilized as the goshawk, the mountain hawk-eagle was highly valued for flights in mountain regions. A common hunting procedure was to walk ridges and hillsides and fly the bird from the fist to quarry

171

hampered by snow. It is worth noting that, although the golden eagle is found in Japan, there is no record of it ever being used by Japanese falconers.

Many of the less commonly utilized eagles are simply not available for falconry purposes in Europe and North America and even attempting to assess their practical value is an almost impossible task. Conclusions can simply not be drawn from odd and isolated European experiences. The success being achieved with captive breeding may one day result in exotic species being a little more frequently employed (and it is interesting that golden eagle hybrids have been produced); until then, judgment is best reserved. That said, I feel the golden eagle's performance and impressive track record will make it a very hard act to follow.

Bibliography

Beebe, F. 1992. *The Complete Falconer*. Hancock House Publishers.

Beebe, F. 1976. *Hawks, Falcons and Falconry*. Hancock House Publishers.

Fentzloff, C. 1979. Chapter 14 *Die Beizjagd*. Paul Parey Publishers.

Fischer, W. 1979. *Stein, Kaffern und Keilschwanz Adler*. Die Neue Brehm-Bucherei.

Harting, J. 1971. *Hints on the management of hawks and practical falconry*. Thames Valley Press edition.

Hollinshead, M. 1993. *Hawking Ground Quarry*. Hancock House Publishers.

Jameson, E. 1962. *The Hawking of Japan*. Published at Davis, California.

Polo, M. 1986 ed. *The Travels of Marco Polo*. Penguin books edition translated and with an introduction by R. Latham.

Remmler, F. 1970/1971. Erinnerungen aus meinem Leben mit Adlern. *Dt. Falkenorden Journal*.

About the Author

Martin Hollinshead has been involved with birds of prey since growing up in Staffordshire, England. Very much a practical falconer, he has flown all of the birds normally associated with ground game, and his first book, *Hawking Ground Quarry* (1993), dealt with the subject thoroughly. His appreciation of and admiration for these birds shine through his work and make *Hawking with Golden Eagles* an interesting and entertaining read.

Martin Hollinshead with a female eagle.   *Photo: J. Hiebeler*

Quality Hancock House Titles

Hawking Ground Quarry
Martin Hollinshead
ISBN 0-88839-320-2

City Peregrines
A Ten-year Saga of
New York City Falcons
Saul Frank
ISBN 0-88839-330-X

The Hunting Falcon
Bruce Haak
ISBN 0-88839-343-1

Pirate of the Plains
Adventures with Prairie
Falcons in the High Desert
Bruce Haak
ISBN 0-88839-306-7

The Compleat Falconer
Frank L. Beebe
ISBN 0-88839-253-2

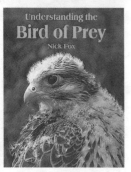

Understanding the
Bird of Prey
Nick Fox
ISBN 0-88839-317-2

Available from Hancock House Publishers
USA: 1431 Harrison Avenue, Blaine, WA 98230-5005
Canada: 19313 Zero Avenue, Surrey, B.C. V4P 1M7
For orders call: 1-800-938-1114 Fax: 1-800-983-2262
Credit cards accepted. Business line: (604) 538-1114

Unsolicited manuscripts accepted for consideration.

hancock

house